GREAT TRAINS OF

EDITED BY P.B.WHITEHOUSE

NORTH AMERICA

PICTURE RESEARCH PATRICIA E. HORNSEY

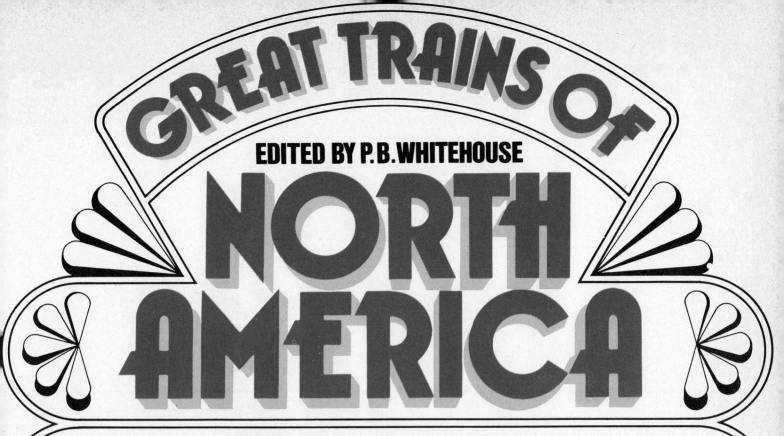

GREAT TRAINS OF

EDITED BY P. B. WHITEHOUSE

NORTH AMERICA

PICTURE RESEARCH PATRICIA E. HORNSEY

CRESCENT BOOKS, NEW YORK

CONTENTS

GREAT TRAINS OF

EDITED BY P. B. WHITEHOUSE

NORTH AMERICA

PICTURE RESEARCH PATRICIA E. HORNSEY

THE FIRST RAILWAYS IN AMERICA

The essential difference between the geographies of Europe and of North America by 1830 was that while in Europe civilisation had existed for centuries, and had established a complex structure of towns, buildings, land ownership, property rights, and other rights-of-way including turnpike roads and canals, through which the railways had to thread themselves, in America a nearly virgin landscape was still being or had only recently been wrested from the red man, and most of the land had no individual owners at all. Turnpike roads and canals had begun to be built, but broad and long the railways could go where they wished without much consideration for other occupiers of the land, since there were none.

Tracks were laid down the main streets of towns — though often enough the tracks were there first and the town later — and they rarely had to build bridges to cross roads. The tendency, especially since money was much scarcer than in Europe, was to build railways quickly and cheaply, and this policy was encouraged by the government, which often granted to the companies large tracts of land in the country to be served by the new line, on condition that trains were running by a given date. The route could always be levelled, straight-

ened, or improved by rebuilding later, and line relocations in the USA are still continuing, although they are quite rare in Europe.

There were a few horse tramways in the Eastern States, built often to act as canal feeders; and it was on one such, the Delaware & Hudson Canal Company's line at Honesdale, Pennsylvania, that the first 'road-service' locomotive in America first ran in 1829. It was the *Stourbridge Lion,* a Killingworth-type engine built in England by Foster & Rastrick of Stourbridge. Unfortunately it was too heavy for the track, and was taken out of service.

Steam locomotion really started in America on the Baltimore & Ohio Railroad, an ambitious project commenced in 1829. During 1831 the railroad company arranged a locomotive contest on similar lines to the one at Rainhill, though with even stricter weight limits, and the main part of the contest consisting of a month's practical service in traffic. Five competitors entered, all American, and the winner was a watchmaker named Phineas Davis, who entered a vertical-boiler four-wheeler. Although it proved an evolutionary dead end, it was quite a practical design up to a certain size and in

fact the last of the 18 similar engines he built for the company stayed at work until 1893. By 1835 steam power ruled the tracks of the B&O to the exclusion of horses, and many other railways were following suit.

Technically, the important difference between American and British railways resulted from the former's lighter and rougher construction, and greater need to save capital outlay. British-type four-wheeled engines and carriages would not stay on the uneven rails, and so they had to be provided with guiding wheels and bogies. This in turn meant that passenger coaches, for instance, had to be built much longer, and the abandonment of compartments in favour of open saloons was then purely a matter of cost saving. On the other hand, the scarcity of bridges and tunnels meant that there was plenty of room to build high and wide, and the steeper gradients put early emphasis on the need to have powerful engines. American locomotive builders, having started by copying Stephenson's Planets, soon developed them greatly, first of all replacing the front carrying wheels by a two-axle bogie, and by the early 1840s had evolved the standard 'Wild West' 4-4-0, a simple, robust and powerful machine which was the commonest motive power unit on American lines until the 1880s.

As early as 1840 the Birmingham & Gloucester Railway in England, faced with the problem of working up the 1 in 37 Lickey Incline and hearing good reports of them from America, ordered 14 typical 4-2-0s from the firm of Norris of Philadelphia. For the rest of the 19th century the development of railways in the world outside Europe and America was, as a rule, in the hands of either British or American engineers and schools of design. British engineers were given a head start by their country's political dominance, but many colonial administrations found the more-basic methods of the Americans better suited to local conditions.

Above: An American Southern Pacific centennial celebration exhibit in 1969 depicting 'Jupiter' (in reality preserved 'Genoa') which hauled the first train from the West to the Golden Spike ceremony in 1869, backed by a modern 3,600hp diesel-electric. Southern Pacific Transportation Co

Below: An 1839 locomotive built by Norris in Philadelphia for the Berlin-Potsdam Railway. DB Film Archiv

Bottom right: Various productions of the Baldwin Company of Philadelphia in the late 1800s. Science Museum London

Facing page: Typical early American domestic product was the 'Wild West' 4-4-0; this exhibit depicts one by William A Lendrum, of Scranton. Science Museum London

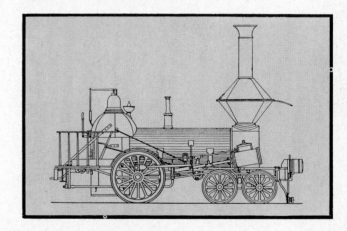

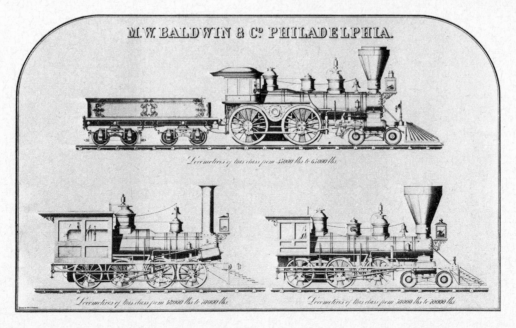

THE PENN CENTRAL

Penn Central, to give the PENN CENTRAL TRANS-
PORTATION COMPANY its popular title, is, like Burlington Northern, a new name in the railway field. Third
in size (based on route mileage) of railways in North
America, it just comes over the 20,000 miles mark, with
BN and Canadian National. There, any comparison with
the other two giants ceases, for, while BN appears quickly
and easily to have consummated its recent merger, and
CN has likewise in its half-century of existence become a
well-run property, Penn Central is a very, very sick railroad.

Before we consider today's situation, it is best to look
at the historical development of Penn Central's components — the New York Central Railroad System (NYC)
and the Pennsylvania Railroad (PRR), whose merger
took place on February 1, 1968. Both constituents were
themselves the result of the combination, over the years,
of many smaller companies.

The name New York Central dates from 1853, when
a number of short lines were linked up and consolidated
to provide a through route between Albany, capital of
New York State, and Buffalo, a gateway city, opposite
Canada's Niagara peninsular. Two links with New York
city, the New York & Harlem and the more-direct New
York & Hudson, were acquired by Commodore
Cornelius Vanderbilt, who had made a fortune from real
estate and ferryboat operation. In 1867, the commodore
consolidated the lines to Albany with the NYC to form
what was to become the New York Central & Hudson
River RR from NY City through to Buffalo. A couple of
years later, he acquired the Lake Shore & Michigan
Southern, which linked Buffalo with Chicago via the
south shore of Lake Erie, Cleveland and Toledo, on an
easily graded route.

Another Vanderbilt component was the Michigan
Central — from Detroit via Kalamazoo to Chicago — and
the associated Canada Southern, a geographically direct
link between Detroit and Buffalo across south-western
Ontario, and north of Lake Erie. A further accretion at
the western end of the developing system was the 'Big
Four' route — the Cleveland, Cincinnati, Chicago & St
Louis. By then the cities served included not only those
named in the last title, but also Columbus and
Indianapolis. All of them were also to be served by the
Pennsylvania RR. The Michigan Central also had a long
rambling secondary main line from Detroit up the east
side of the upper Michigan peninsula, via Bay City to
Mackinan City. The latter was also served by a similar
offshoot of the Pennsylvania, the Grand Rapids &
Indiana RR, up the west side of the peninsula, from Fort
Wayne.

A further important link gave the NYC access to
Boston — the Boston & Albany, which facilitated passenger traffic between Boston and points west of Albany
and made many important freight connections to New
England. The NYC also acquired erstwhile rivals. The
New York, West Shore & Buffalo was built up the
western bank of the Hudson river, from Weehawken,
New Jersey, opposite New York city. A rate war ensued,
the West Shore went bankrupt, and the NYC acquired it.
Today, the West Shore line, singled, is still an important
supplementary freight route to and from the New York
metropolitan area; cross-river connection was by ferry
and car float.

**Top: The Buffalo Day Express of the Pennsylvania Railroad
crossing the Susa river into Harrisburg. Pa, in May 1963.
W E Zullig**

10

Two major constituents remain to be mentioned. Much the busier is the Pittsburgh & Lake Erie; its importance is quite out of proportion to its small mileage, for it serves the competitive Pittsburgh industrial area, with its many steel plants and heavy coal traffic. The P & LE is one prosperous corner of PC. The last line to mention is the Rome, Watertown & Ogdensburg; it linked the Niagara Falls area, Syracuse and Utica with Massena in northern New York state, where connection was made with the Grand Trunk (now CN) so providing a through route to Montreal.

So much for the New York Central, which extensively served Ohio, Indiana, Michigan and Illinois as well as its name state. The Pennsylvania also grew to serve *its* name-state and the four other states just mentioned, and the Philadelphia-Baltimore-Washington so-called corridor as well. Although the corridor is the busiest of PRR's passenger routes, the system's main line is the route that leaves the New York-Washington line at North Philadelphia and heads west via Paoli, Harrisburg and Pittsburgh (for Chicago and St Louis). Dating as a through rail route from 1858, the main line is heavily graded as it climbs the Allegheny mountains, and includes the spectacular Horseshoe curve.

The PRR was conceived and financed from Philadelphia, at one time the largest and most important American city. It was the threat of either New York or Baltimore becoming a rival port for traffic to and from the developing American West that made finance available for the building of the PRR. The line expanded to the west of Pittsburgh through several subsidiaries. The Pittsburgh, Fort Wayne & Chicago, again a consolidation of several small lines, provided the western link in an alternative (to the NYC) New York — Chicago route. The Vandalia Line — the Terre Haute & Indianapolis RR — gave access to St Louis. Another major western constituent was the Pittsburgh, Cincinnati, Chicago & St Louis Railway; with yet others, they provided the PRR with a comprehensive network of lines west of Pittsburgh, thoroughly intertwined with NYC routes in the same area.

In the east, the picture, at least viz-a-viz the NYC, was rather different, for the NYC served only to a small degree the states of Pennsylvania and New Jersey. The PRR had other competitors — the Reading System, and the Baltimore & Ohio. It, too, acquired a number of smaller eastern roads. Among these were the United RRs of New Jersey (in the Philadelphia area), the Northern Central with a north-south route out of Baltimore which penetrated the NYC's territory to reach the shores of Lake Ontario at Sodus Point, the West Jersey RR (to Cape May), and the Camden & Atlantic — Philadelphian's short route to the seaside (and, in the heyday of steam, site of some very smart running with Atlantic-type locomotives).

The route to Atlantic City has other features of interest. It forms the core of a relatively rare American phenomenon, a joint railway — the Pennsylvania — Reading Seashore Lines. The Camden — Atlantic City — Cape May area was served by parallel overlapping lines of both the PRR and the Reading System. In the aftermath of the economic depression, the two groups of lines were placed under common management and much of the duplication was eliminated. Even today, services in the area are provided by Budd diesel railcars lettered 'Pennsylvania Reading Seashore Lines'.

Bottom: Pennsy's diesel-headed Baltimore Day Express at Rockville in May 1963. W E Zullig

11

The PRR and the NYC brought just under 10,000 route miles each to the new Penn Central system. A third, important but smaller, constituent included from the start of 1969 was the New York, New Haven & Hartford RR. The New Haven was already bankrupt, having been so since the early nineteen-sixties, but a condition of the P-C merger, imposed by the Interstate Commerce Commission (ICC) was that PC took responsibility for it. The New Haven brought over 1,600 additional route-miles to the system, including the 230-mile-long main line — the so-called shore line — between New York and Boston, as well as a number of branches of varying importance in Southern New England. In addition there was the important freight-only route between the Maybrook, NY, gateway (with links to the south and west) and New Haven, Conn.

The New York, New Haven & Hartford RR, in addition to serving the area indicated by its title, expanded in the decades from 1890, by taking over a number of other fairly small systems. Its shore line extended beyond New Haven to New London, whence the New York, Providence & Boston RR continued to Providence, RI, to connect with the Old Colony RR. The Old Colony linked Providence with Boston and had a small network east of the route serving Cape Cod. Another important constituent was the New York & New England RR, extending from Fishkill (on the Hudson, 60 miles above New York) via Hartford, Willimantic and Readville, to Boston. Other sectors of the New Haven include the Housatonic System from Bridgeport north to Pittsfield, and the Connecticut River RR, north from Springfield with connections to Canada.

The sub-components of the three PC constituents had largely, by the turn of the century, become consolidated in varying degrees to the three major systems. The New York Central and the Pennsylvania became great rivals. Serving the most developed areas of the United States, their train services and frequencies were more akin to those in Europe than those of the railroads which served the west, where sparse population, vast distances and limitations on capital meant infrequent service and rough tracks. (Later, the position was to be reversed.)

The Central and the Pennsylvania vied with each other in many fields, quality of rolling stock, competitive trains between common points, in particular New York and Chicago, and in presenting a public image which spoke for itself. Both railways carried out many improvements and consolidated their positions. Even by 1891, the Central had a four-track main line between Albany and Buffalo, and indeed, by the combination of routes, there were four tracks all the way from New York City to Chicago, about 960 miles.

Much of the Central's consolidation, after Commodore Vanderbilt's death in 1877, was carried out by his son, William H Vanderbilt. It was William who first used the phrase 'the public be damned', when being questioned by a reporter over services to Chicago. The expression still has a familiar ring today!

In Edwardian times, the Central invested heavily in a great new terminal — Grand Central — in New York City. Train operations were on two levels, both underground, and were served by a sizeable suburban electrification scheme, using the protected third rail dc system.

Left: PRR Class Mp54 electric mu of Penn Central at Philadelphia 30th Street in July 1971. V Goldberg

Pennsylvania Railroad passenger diesel No 9542 descending Horsehoe curve, Altoona, Pa. J M Jarvis

Harmon, 33 miles from New York City, was the change-over point between steam and electric traction for long-distance trains; suburban services have mainly been worked by multiple-unit trains. The Central built many fine stations (sometimes jointly) in the twentieth century. Albany, Cleveland, Buffalo and Cincinatti come to mind, each a different expression of the importance of passenger service.

Grand Central was also the New York terminal for all New Haven suburban services, and for most of its long-distance trains, but the spectacular Hell Gate bridge high-level route to Penn station in Manhattan was used to give connections to points south and west. The New Haven also embraced electrification in the Edwardian era, but selected an overhead-wire 11,000V ac system, making it necessary to dual-equip electric mus and loco-motives since the approach to Grand Central, being NYC owned, was electrified third-rail dc. The electrification extended as far as New Haven, 72 miles. The branches to New Canaan and Danbury were also electrified. The New Haven intended to extend its electrification beyond the end of its four-track main line at New Haven through Boston, but its finances did not permit it.

The Pennsylvania also carried out substantial improvements in Edwardian times. In place of its ferry-served terminal in Jersey City, opposite Manhattan, it extended under the Hudson river in tunnel to a 28-acre site in mid-town New York, the new Penn station. The extension did not stop there, but continued on in tunnels under the East River to Long Island. There,

connection was made with the Hell Gate bridge route, and hence to the New Haven permitting through services from the south to Boston. Sunnyside PRR car storage yard in the borough of Queens was also served, and the PRR obtained control of Long Island RR, many of whose trains were extended to Penn station, much more convenient than its own terminals east of the East River.

The initial Pennsylvania river tunnel electrification was third-rail dc, but a few years later, suburban electrification in the Philadelphia area was carried out at 11,000V ac 25Hz, with overhead contact. The same system was later adopted for main-line work, and by the late nineteen-thirties, it was in use between New York and Washington, and west as far as Harrisburg on the main line. Eventually, about 660 route-miles were electrified and are still in use today. The famous GGI streamline locomotive class was developed in the thirties for the electrified lines.

Many of the express trains on Penn Central's constituents carried famous names. Between New York and Chicago, the New York Central had the longer, but easier route — indeed the term 'Water Level Route' was much used in advertising. The Pennsylvania had tough grades west of Philadelphia, but measured only 908 miles to Chicago, compared with the Central's 960 miles. Running time between the two cities was reduced from 28 hours to 20 hours in 1902. The Twentieth Century Limited (of the Central) and the Pennsylvania Special (from 1912, the Broadway Limited) were the rivals, and the schedule was reduced to 18 hours for both in 1905.

At intervals, each train was re-equipped with the finest and latest in rolling stock. In the 'twenties and 'thirties, the Central's famous Hudsons and the Pennsy's Class K4 Pacifics, were main-stays of express passenger motive power while steam was king. In 1938, streamlined equipment was introduced on both trains, both on a new 16-hour schedule. Diesel traction followed in post-war years, together with more new train sets.

The New Haven, too, had its crack expresses, the Merchants Limited, the Yankee Clipper and the Bay State; all (at one time) were all-parlour car trains, ie all first-class day accommodation for the main New York – Boston run.

During the 1939-45 war, all railroads carried phenomenal passenger loads, and large orders for streamlined equipment were placed after the war, to meet the hoped-for continuation of the boom. Air competition (and new highways) decreed otherwise. The railroads appeared to be slow to appreciate the erosion of their traffic. Certainly, it was *not* the case that no traffic survived; rather, the railroads failed to act to hold traffic in those fields – the shorter distances – where they could continue to compete effectively. Losses on long-distance services seemed to lead to a lack of faith in all

services, and during 'sixties, there was a rapid decline in punctuality, cleanliness, staff courtesy and maintenance. Management appeared to have completely lost heart.

It is on Penn Central's constituents that most of the blame for the bad image nationally of all railroad passenger service in recent years must fall, serving as they did, New York, nerve-centre of the country's communications. To the writer of these words, albeit a visitor from abroad, it was clear in the 'sixties that all three component railroads were in a serious decline, with major deficiencies in management and maintenance. It is all the more surprising that the ICC should approve the merger of such obviously ailing operations, and accept the specious arguments in support of it put forward by the railroads' managements.

The outcome was a shock more to the financial world than to the serious student of railways – bankruptcy from June 21, 1970. The subsequent disclosures of corruption and incompetence in mangement have been dealt with in the book *Wreck of the Penn Central*. The story revealed is not a creditable one. Intercompany strife, incompetence, personality clashes, trade union intransigence, job feather-bedding, plain corruption in the financial field – all were to be found in Penn Central.

BURLINGTON NORTHERN

The name BURLINGTON NORTHERN is a newcomer to the American railway scene. It dates only from March 2, 1970, when three major railways, and certain other lines, were merged. The railways involved were the Chicago, Burlington & Quincy Railroad (Burlington Route — 8,500 miles), the Great Northern Railway (route of the Empire Builder — 8,260 miles) and the Northern Pacific Railway ('Main Street of the North-West' — 6,780 miles). Also included were the Spokane, Portland & Seattle Railway — 950 miles) and the Pacific Coast Railroad — 32 miles.

The merger had been proposed more than once over the years and was finally approved only after prolonged inquiry by the Interstate Commerce Commission — the United States Federal regulatory body for transport. There had, however, for many years been interlinking ownership between the various companies involved. The GN and NP owned jointly the CB&Q, although the latter was larger than either of its parents. The GN and NP also owned jointly the SP&S, which was geographically quite separate from the CB&Q. The CB&Q and SP&S were also operated quite separately, with their own individual managements.

With over 24,500 miles of route, Burlington Northern is second only to Canadian National Railways in size of system in North America, with Penn Central a poor (literally!) third.

Each of the three major components of BN included numerous short, local, or bigger constituents, but the first to achieve major system status was the Northern Pacific. After the choice for the first transcontinental railroad fell to the central route, that is, the one followed by the Union Pacific and Central Pacific to San Francisco, for which a charter was granted in 1862, pressure continued for the alternative route to be built.

A further charter was granted in 1864, in the midst of the American Civil War, but construction of the Northern Pacific route, from both ends, began only in 1870. The eastern end started at Carlton, near Duluth. Minnesota, and the western end started, northwards initially, from the Columbia river, near Portland, Oregon.

Bismark, ND, and Tacoma, Wash, had been reached from east and west respectively when a national financial crisis caused suspension of construction in 1873. Work resumed in 1879, and the transcontinental route of the NP of 2,260 miles was finally completed in 1883. New construction and acquisition brought the NP route mileage to about 6,780 at the time of the BN merger. The main line, one that is still largely (and unusually) signalled by semaphores, runs from the Twin Cities of St Paul — Minneapolis via Fargo, Bismark, Mandon and Billings to Butte. At Butte is one of the world's largest open-pit copper mines, served by the Butte, Anacondo & Pacific Railway, which until recently had electric traction. In the same area there is an alternative more-northerly loop of the NP serving Helena, State capital of Montana. The two routes rejoin at Garrison, Mont, and the main line continues west to Spokane, Wash. A south-westerly course takes the route on to Pasco, Wash, through most of Washington State's fertile country, and so to the Puget Sound at Tacoma. From there tracks fork north to Seattle and south to Portland.

The NP had several important secondary routes. From the Twin Cities, a line led up to the two lakehead ports, Duluth and Superior, which also had a direct route to the west via Brainerd to link with the main transcontinental route to Staples. A little to the west of Staples, and still in Minnesota, the NP had a route via Grand Forks to Winnipeg, in Canada. North Dakota was served by a number of branch lines. In Montana, a huge

Restaurant car named 'Lake Michigan' in BN livery at Grand Forks in July 1972.
V Goldberg

state ('Big Sky Country') which takes a whole day to cross (the rail mileage is about 760), Livingston acts as gateway to the Yellowstone National Park. Westward from there, the main line follows a scenic route through the Big Belt and Bitter Root ranges of the Rocky Mountains. Much of the route west follows the trail of the Lewis and Clark expedition of 1804, particularly up the Yellowstone river in Montana.

The NP's 'herald', or crest, was unusual. An annular ring containing the words Northern Pacific surrounded a monad — a Chinese mystical symbol formed by a circle split into two equal parts by an S-shaped line. One half was black, the other red. The symbol appears to date from the inauguration of NP's crack train, the North Coast Limited, in 1900. The eight-car train had electric lighting and represented the peak of wooden carriage construction.

The North Coast Limited required six sets of equipment to maintain service and some new stock was acquired in 1909 and 1930, but the first major delivery of streamlined cars did not appear until 1947-8. In 1954 20 dome cars, both coaches (second-class) and sleepers, were acquired, to be followed by buffet-lounge cars in 1955 and six new diners in 1958. Finally, in 1959 slumber coaches (each named after a Scottish loch) were added, to make economy-class sleeping accommodation available. The various additions to stock during the 1950s permitted the second-line transcontinental train, the Mainstreeter, to be re-equipped, although latterly this train was formed of only five or six cars.

Northern Pacific passenger services were almost entirely dropped when the government-financed organisation AMTRAK took over responsibility, but political pressures soon brought back service over the NP main line, three days a week, on a 'trial' basis.

The Great Northern Railway had its beginnings in the St Paul & Pacific Railway, which had become moribund, after starting to build north-westward out of St Paul. A young Ontario-born man, James Jerome Hill, moved to the west in 1856, intent on trading with the Orient. Instead, he became involved in river transport on the Mississippi, and later gained control of the St Paul & Pacific. With vigour he extended the line up to the Canadian border at Pembina, to which point the Canadian Pacific built a link south from Winnipeg. Incidentally, until 1883, Jim Hill was also associated with the Canadian Pacific Railway.

The St Paul-Winnipeg link prospered, and Hill resolved to extend westward to the Pacific Ocean. The new line followed a route between the Canadian border and the line of the Northern Pacific and was well engineered. The title Great Northern was adopted in 1890. In 1893, the line reached the Puget sound at Everett, Wash, 33 miles north of Seattle. The route reached a summit of 5,213ft above sea level, 12 miles west of Glacier Park station, and only 55 miles of route was higher than 4,000, an important consideration when winter snows are remembered.

The GN crossing of the Cascade mountains was greatly improved in 1929 when the original Cascade tunnel (2⅔ miles) was replaced with one 7¾ miles long. The new tunnel formed part of a new 73-mile electrification at 11,500-volt 25-Herz alternating current, which replaced an earlier three-phase system. The later electrification was in turn discontinued in 1956 when diesel

traction took over. Another major new tunnel and lengthy re-alignment of the GN route (by then, in fact Burlington Northern) took place in 1970 with the construction of the Libby dam, in Western Montana.

On the west coast, the GN had its main line from Seattle through Everett to the Canadian border at Blaine, and thence into Canada, partly over tracks shared with Canadian National, to its own station in Vancouver. The GN station was demolished in the late 1960s, after GN trains had been transferred to the CNR station. After a year (1971/2) during which the line was without passenger trains, international service was reintroduced under AMTRAK sponsorship in July 1972.

At its easterly end, the GN reached Chicago over tracks of the CB&QRR (as did the NP). Between St Paul and Minot, ND (almost 500 miles), the GN possessed two separate routes, and its branch-line coverage in northern North Dakota was particularly complete, with over a dozen separate lines to the north, but all of them stopping short of the Canadian border. The representation of these on a map has given rise to the term 'picket fence country'. As with the NP, the GN had links from the twin lakehead ports both to the Twin Cities and to Crookston, Minn, on the Winnipeg line, and Grand Forks on the transcontinental route.

Ex-Northern Pacific East Coast Limited at
Billings in July 1970. V Goldberg

Jim Hill's construction of the GN without Federal land grants (in contrast to the NP), and his vigour in encouraging settlement of immigrants in the country through which the GN passed, earned him the title of Empire Builder — the name also given to the principal transcontinental GN train in 1929, when it was refurbished. The Empire Builder was successor to the Oriental Limited, dating from 1905, which had a maritime extension in the form of the GN steamship *Minnesota* (20,000 tons) linking Seattle with Japan and China. A further marine venture was the Great Northern Pacific Steamship Co (jointly owned by the GN and NP), which in 1915 inaugurated a service between Portland and San Francisco. The voyage took 30 hours, three hours less than the competing Southern Pacific's train!

The Empire Builder train joined the ranks of the streamliners in 1947, when five new train sets (four owned by GN, one by the CB&Q) entered service, having been ordered in 1943, but delayed by the war. The schedule of the new trains was 45 hours between Chicago and the Pacific Northwest, 13½ hours less than former timings. A further five new 15-car trains entered service in 1951, at which time the 1947 equipment and one further new train made up another revised and slightly slower schedule by the Western Star. In 1955, 22

dome cars (six of them full-length Great Dome lounge cars) were added to the fleet. Both trains continued until the advent of AMTRAK, which maintained operation of the Empire Builder, but via Milwaukee in the East and rerouted over the former NP line to Seattle west of Spokane.

The first Empire Builder streamlined trains introduced a colourful livery of bands of orange and green, separated by gold striping. In the 1960s the GN introduced its Big Sky Blue livery, but it had by no means been fully applied by the time of the BN merger, when a green livery was adopted.

Other GN passenger services operated until the formation of AMTRAK included the picturesquely named Badger and Gopher trains linking the Twin Cities with Duluth-Superior, and a Grand Forks Winnipeg train making connections with the Western Star at Grand Forks.

Although we have given prominence to the passenger services of both GN and NP, population along both lines has been relatively sparse, and both roads have been predominantly freight carriers, with freight revenue far outstripping that from passengers. Forest products, agriculture and mines are the main sources of freight traffic, while NP was also a major land-owner.

The Chicago, Burlington & Quincy Railroad, or Burlington Lines as it was known with its subsidiaries, was rather different. Although its mileage was greater than either of its parents — GN and NP acquired joint control in 1908 — it did not reach the Pacific. It did, however, form a latter-day link in the transcontinental route followed by the famed California Zephyr train, which, west of Denver, used the Denver & Rio Grande Western's short line to Salt Lake City. West from the Mormon capital, the tracks of the johnny-come-lately Western Pacific, completed only in 1909, were used to reach the Pacific Ocean, or rather, the San Francisco Bay area at Oakland.

The CB&Q had its beginnings in the Aurora Branch Railroad, a spur off the short Galena & Chicago Union, which became the foundation of the CB&Qs rival, the Chicago & North Western Railway. The Aurora built west first to the Mississippi river (it adopted the title Chicago, Burlington & Quincy Railroad in 1855), forming a link with the Missouri river at St Joseph, via a ferry at Quincy, Ill, and thence the Hannibal & St Joseph Railroad. A more northerly crossing of the Missouri was later made at Council Bluffs, Ia (reached in 1870), whence the main line stretched west to Denver, 1,034 miles from Chicago. Other routes reached south to St Louis and to Kansas City; north from Aurora to the Twin Cities of Minneapolis-St Paul; and two lines to the north-west — one from Lincoln, Neb, the other from Denver, to reach Billings, Mont, on the NP Main line, where a GN branch was also met.

Of the Denver-Billings route, the 238 miles from Denver to Wendover, Wyo, form the northern end of the Colorado & Southern Railway. Of the Southern's 718 miles, the 589 miles south from Wendover to the Texas-New Mexico state line form part of a cross-country link from Denver to the Gulf of Mexico at Galveston, Tex. The 792 miles from Texline to Galveston are part of the 1,362-mile Forth Worth & Denver Railway, owned by the C&S. The C&S, in turn has been controlled by the CB&Q since 1909. An interesting part, for a time, of the C&S system was the narrow-gauge (3ft) Denver, South

Park & Pacific Railroad, built through rugged scenic country, south-west from Denver, as a rival to the D&RGW to tap Colorado's mines. Apart from one short spur, which was converted to standard gauge during 1939-45, the last leg of the DSP&PRR, between Denver and Leadville, closed in 1937. The C&S and FW&D are controlled by – but not part of – BN.

Although the Burlington (as the CB&Q was often called) was a leader in the western railroad passenger field, it, too, derived most of its income from freight. The Burlington's best-known contribution to the passenger market is probably the Zephyr title, afterwards carried by a whole fleet of high-speed trains. The pioneer Zephyr introduced in 1934 brought stainless steel carbody construction, and successful diesel-electric traction, to the railroads. While the early articulated trains became an embarrassment due to their limited capacity, the basic designs were developed, and today's General Motors diesel locomotives and Budd stainless-steel passenger cars are the consequences of those early efforts.

Zephyr raced in all directions, from Chicago to the Twin Cities, from Denver to Dallas (Texas Zephyr) and on many other routes. The Denver Zephyr, with two full-length train sets built in 1936, was one of the most successful. In 1956 the two 12-car trains were replaced by new stock, the last completely new train sets to be built for US service until the advent of the Metroliners and experimental Turbotrains. Today, the route of the Denver Zephyr is still served by AMTRAK's San Francisco Zephyr which proceed from Denver over the Union Pacific to Ogden, and then over the Southern Pacific to Oakland.

The original trackage of the CB&Q between Chicago and Aurora is, in addition, served by double-deck Gallery cars in commuter service, over a three-track section of the line.

The Spokane Portland & Seattle Railway provides a 380-mile short cut, via the north bank of the Columbia river, for the GN and NP, from Spokane, Wash, to Portland, Ore. The latter-day twice-daily (in each direction) passenger train service provided connections with both transcontinental trains of both the NP and the GN. The SP&S itself owns two subsidiaries, the Oregon Trunk Railway from Wishram, Wash, to Bend, Ore, and the Oregon Electric Railway (no longer electrified) from Portland to Eugene, Ore. One small line, the Pacific Coast Railroad serving industries in the Seattle area, rounds off the Burlington Northern system.

Above: Head end of a Burlington Route . train of the Chicago Burlington & Quincy RR at Colorado Springs in June 1964. V Goldberg

Top: Ex-Great Northern GP diesel-electric locomotive No 1521 in July 1970. V Goldberg

UNION PACIFIC, SOUTHERN PACIFIC & SANTA FE

The Centenary of the completion of the first transcontinental railway across the United State of America has but recently been celebrated by the **UNION PACIFIC RAILROAD** and its guests – the Golden Spike was driven at Promontory Point, west of Ogden, Utah, on May 10, 1869. Much has been written of the original construction of that most important main line. Suffice it to say here that today's route from Omaha, Neb, or rather Council Bluffs, Iowa, on the east bank of the Missouri river, to Ogden (about 994 miles) is a very different property from the pioneer route of 1869. Among the busiest of any main lines west of Chicago, it is the core of the Union Pacific system; over the years it has been constantly improved, with double tracks throughout (often on seperate formations to follow flatter gradients), easier curves, and several generations of mammoth motive power units of different types.

The Union Pacific, despite its ideal geographical position, does not, on its own, meet the definition transcontinental, nor does it extend from Chicago to the Pacific coast – not, that is, on this 'central' route. Chicago is reached over the tracks of the Milwaukee Road, which is a transcontinental route in its own right, and the Pacific, at San Francisco bay, is reached over Southern Pacific tracks west of Ogden. The whole forms the famed Overland Route, once served by such popular trains as the City of San Francisco, the Overland Limited, the Pacific Limited and the San Francisco Challenger. Until 1955, the Chicago & North Western Railway was used between Chicago and Omaha; possible merger plans at present being considered could transfer UP traffic to the Rock Island Lines between those two points.

Union Pacific's 9,000 miles of route include many other main lines. Among the earliest of them was the Denver Pacific, a relatively short branch from the main line at Cheyenne to the then burgeoning city of Denver, 106 miles away, and completed in 1870. Later, Denver was to have a more direct UP route to the east, joining the original transcontinental route at Julesburg, 197 miles from Denver, in the extreme north-east corner of Colorado. This was the route taken by the streamliner City of Denver, which competed with Burlington's Denver Zephyr for Chicago-Denver traffic. Another early component was the Kansas Pacific, a 640-mile route from Denver to Kansas City and thence east to St Louis over the Wabash Railway (now part of the Norfolk & Western). Over this route ran the streamliner City of St Louis, later the City of Kansas City.

Subsequently, UP put out its own links to reach the Pacific coast. First came the Oregon Short Line, leaving the main transcontinental route at Granger, Wyoming, and heading north-west through Pocatello (214 miles) and Hinkle (756 miles) to Portland (940 miles). From Portland, UP tracks head north a further 183 miles to Seattle, via Tacoma. Both Portland and Seattle are important ports, and also interchange points with other railroads serving the north-west Pacific area. Union Pacific reaches other major sources of traffic by major branch lines. From Pocaletto, the mines at Butte (263 miles) are served, as well as West Yellowstone, while from Hinkle, the city of Spokane (191 miles) and Washington's agricultural area are reached, as well as Yakima, centre of a fruit-growing belt.

Last of UP's major links is the Los Angeles & Salt Lake, which brought UP service to Southern California. From Ogden, the route serves the Utah state capital of Salt Lake City, only 36 miles south of Ogden, before crossing the great deserts of Utah and Nevada as it runs south-west via Las · Vegas – the gambling city of Southern Nevada. It reaches the Los Angeles area after crossing the spectacular Cajon pass. This 821-mile extension brought UP to tidewater on its own tracks, and also gave access to the industries and major fruit and vegetable growing areas around Los Angeles.

The early years of Union Pacific were somewhat chequered. The scandals of the Credit Mobilier – the original construction company – are long since passed, but by no means forgotten. Then the UP went into receivership in 1893, but by the turn of the century, many physical improvements were in hand. UP became part of the Harriman empire. With its strategically located trunk main line, the railroad could hardly avoid being profitable; lengthy freight trains of 100 vehicles, 10,000 tons in weight and a mile or more long can today be seen at half-hourly or hourly intervals between Omaha and Ogden.

Notwithstanding the heavy and profitable freight traffic, a fleet of streamlined passenger trains developed from modest beginnings in the mid-nineteen-thirties. Named City trains linked Chicago with Denver, Portland, San Francisco and Los Angeles. Sporting a bright yellow livery, with bold red lettering, the UP Passenger train was a striking sight. As costs rose and passenger service contracted, the four city trains were consolidated one by one, until finally a single combined train was operated with through cars to each city. In summer, the City could load to 23 cars, with five diesel locomotives providing 12,000hp for a train nearly half-a-mile long. High standards were maintained by UP until service passes to AMTRAK, which has largely concentrated on other routes. The current San Francisco Zephyr, which uses UP tracks only between Denver, Cheyenne and Ogden, is now the only passenger train over UP rails.

SOUTHERN PACIFIC LINES extend over about 14,000 route miles, a figure which exceeded that of the Santa Fe only as a result of its recent acquisition of control of the Cotton Belt line – the St Louis-Southwestern Railway, in which SP has had a majority holding since 1932. Southern Pacific Lines is the title used by the Southern Pacific Transportation Company for its railway operations; SPT Co also operates pipelines and highway freight services. SP is already well past its centenary, having had its origins in the Sacramento Valley RR, which extended 21 miles east from Sacramento, California, and was opened in 1855 to serve the gold camps in the foothills of the Sierra Nevada mountains.

Union Pacific Railroad's No 6900, certainly when introduced in 1969, and probably still, the biggest diesel locomotive ever built on a single frame. It follows the UP tradition of outstandingly powerful engines – Union Pacific Railroad Company

The first major segment of the SP was the Central Pacific RR. Chartered originally only to build that portion of the first transcontinental railway within the State of California, CP build east from Sacramento, climbed the Sierra Nevada rising to the rim of the canyon of the American river, surmounted Donner pass, then crossed into Nevada, following the Humboldt river. It passed into Utah and finally met the Union Pacific to the north of the Great Salt Lake at Promontory. The four main financial backers of the Central Pacific — Charles Crocker, Mark Hopkins, Collis P Huntington and Leland Stanford — turned to building and acquiring other lines in California, and so built up the SP, which leased the CP in 1885.

The Southern Pacific forms part of two other transcontinental routes. The most southerly, the Sunset route, extends from New Orleans via El Paso, Tucson and Phoenix to Los Angeles, 2,033 miles. In 1894, SP inaugurated the Sunset Limited over the route, and the train took 58 hours from New Orleans to Los Angeles. In contrast to the high altitudes of the other transcontinental lines, the Sunset route skirts the Salton sea in Southern California, 202 feet *below* sea level. West of El Pasco, the Sunset route is shared by trains of the Golden State route, which use the SP line north-east out of El Paso to Tucumcari (331 miles) in north-east New Mexico, where an end-on junction is made with the Rock Island Lines from Chicago via Kansas City.

South of the San Francisco Bay area, Southern Pacific has two quite separate routes to Los Angeles. From the city itself, the coast route goes south via San Jose (47 miles), to which point commuter service is operated, over Paso Robles and then via San Luis Obispo and Santa Barbara to Los Angeles, 470 miles. For over 100 miles, the line is within sight of the Pacific ocean. The alternative route starts from Oakland, across the bay

from San Francisco, and proceeds east, skirting San Pablo bay and Suisun bay before turning south into the San Joaquin valley, via Merced and Fresno to Bakersfield (313 miles). There, the easy grades end and the line climbs to the summit loop built around a cone-shaped hill, to gain height in the Tehachapi mountains (3,967ft) before crossing the western end of the Mojave Desert, and descending to Los Angeles (479 miles). The last few miles from Burbank are shared with the coastal route.

North from San Francisco, or rather Oakland, SP has its Shasta route (parallel to the coast, but well inland) which takes it through the Redwood forests of Northern California and Oregon to Portland, 712 miles. The Shasta route included an important alternative route to the east of the original line over Grants pass — the Cascade line via Klamath Falls, completed in 1927. The new line is about 25 miles shorter than the old Siskiyou line.

Across the Golden Gate and north from Marin country up the Northern Californian coast is another member of the SP family, the Northwestern Pacific Railroad, It is an amalgam of a number of small companies, some of which operated commuter services in the bay area, with ferry links to San Francisco, until the opening of the Golden Gate bridge killed off the traffic. The SP gained control of the NWP in 1929, and maintained passenger service over the northern end of the line, between Willits and Eureka, until the advent of AMTRAK in May 1971. Latterly, the service was but twice weekly, worked by a solitary railcar, but it provided access to the isolated Eel River valley.

The SP had a number of other rail interests, including certain electrically operated lines. Two branch lines south-west of Portland were electrified in 1912-14, but electric services there ceased in 1929. In the San Francisco bay area, some of the NWP commuter lines

were electrified in 1903, and discontinued in 1941 while in the east bay area, around Oakland, several lines electrified in 1911-12 were also abandoned in 1941. Much the largest of the electrified systems was the Pacific Electra Railway, extending over 520 miles of route. The SP gained control in 1911, by which time the PER was already changing from an inter-urban to a suburban operation, as the area it served rapidly developed. Its value to SP was largely as a freight feeder from all over the greater Los Angeles area. Cut-backs in PER passenger service began before the 1939-45 war. Very heavy wartime traffic stemmed the decline, but contraction continued after the war, the last passenger service having closed in 1963.

Perhaps the early opting out of local passenger traffic was a portent of the future long-distance trains, for by the early nineteen-sixties, SP's disenchantment with passengers had become very evident. And that despite its fleet of streamlined named trains – the Coast and Valley Daylights, the Shasta, the Cascade and others – on which standards had once been very high. Service was deliberately downgraded; restaurant and sleeping cars were withdrawn even from trains with journeys extending over two nights. This wanton behaviour eventually attracted official notice and permission for further discontinuances was refused by the regulatory bodies on the ground that substantial traffic had been deliberately discouraged by the deterioration of standards.

Today AMTRAK provides service over four different SP routes. The Coast Daylight is operated daily between Los Angeles and Oakland (for San Francisco and via San Jose). Thrice-weekly service is offered on the other routes – the Sunset between Los Angeles and New Orleans, the Coast Starlight between Portland and Oakland, and the San Francisco Zephyr, between Oakland and Chicago, the last-named train operating daily in summer.

THE ATCHISON, TOPEKA & SANTE FE RAILWAY had its beginnings in Kansas, which state granted it a charter to build to the Colarado state line in 1859. Only with a spur of a substantial land grant – with a time limit of 10 years – did construction get under way in 1868. Starting from the state capital, Topeka, (66 miles west of Kansas City), Dodge City became end-of-line in 1871, and the Colorado state line was reached in 1872. The Atchison & Topeka, as the line was then known, played a major part in the settlement of Kansas, and its colonisation agents sought potential farmers in the Mennonites, a Russian religious sect, among others.

Although the town of Sante Fe, capital of New Mexico, became the next goal, the main line bypassed it, as construction proceeded across South-east Colorado to Albuquerque, and the capital was served by a short branch line from Lamy. To reach Albuquerque, the Raton pass, near the New Mexico-Colorado state line, had to be surmounted. The physical problems there, however, were second to those presented by the young and expanding Denver & Rio Grande, which at that period was still aiming south from Denver; later, it was to head west, into the Rockies.

Battles, both physical and legal, ensued; the Santa Fe won and its first train surmounted Raton at the end of 1878. With its title extended to Atchison, Topeka & Santa Fe, the railway looked even farther west. The Southern Pacific, however, considered New Mexico to be its own territory, and opposed the expansion plans. The Santa Fe parried by obtaining an interest in a charter owned by the St Louis and San Francisco RR. Further legal exercises ensued, but finally the Santa Fe was able to build through to the Pacific coast, completing its line to Los Angeles in 1887.

At its eastern end, acquisitions and new construction brought the Santa Fe to Chicago. Included there was the Chicago & St Louis RR, whose line from Chicago to Streator, Illinois, 90 miles, provided the entry link to the big city. The Santa Fe stretched 2,224 miles from Chicago to Los Angeles. Later construction brought the Santa Fe to San Francisco bay, at Oakland. From Barstow, the line ran to Bakesfield and thence down the San Joaquin valley via Stockton and Richmond, to a terminal at Oakland, 454 miles from Barstow.

From Chicago to Los Angeles, the main line today is double track throughout, except where an alternative route is available, that is, between Newton, Kansas, and the Albuquerque area, and between Los Angeles and San Bernardino, California. The original main line has summits at Raton (7,622ft), Glorietta (7,421ft), Continental Divide (7,247ft) and Arizona Divide (7,313ft). The alternative main line via Amarillo, Texas, 46 miles longer, has a summit level of only 6,470ft at Mountainair. The majority of passenger trains used the old main line via La Junta, which initially had been built to Pueblo, Colorado, before the extensions into New Mexico had left Pueblo on a 64-mile-long branch from La Junta. Pueblo gave connections to the Colorado mining areas, and eventually by joint trackage and running agreements to Denver. Other western extensions took the Santa Fe to San Diego and to El Paso, both points with Mexican connections.

Apart from its coverage in the far south-west, the Santa Fe also served much of Texas, and reached the Gulf of Mexico. From Newton, Kansas, on the main line, a 200-mile-long extension leads to Oklahoma City, and from there (over the rails of the subsidiary Gulf, Colorado & Santa Fe Railway) Forth Worth, Dallas, Houston and the port of Galveston are reached. Western Texas is served by another subsidiary, the Panhándle and Santa Fe Railway. Together, the Santa Fe system covers 13,000 miles of route; until the recent advent of Penn Central and Burlington Northern, it was the longest rail system in the USA. Serving areas which are economically still expanding, and with a high proportion of long-haul and high-rated traffic, the Santa Fe is a prosperous and well-kept railway.

In the middle nineteen-fifties, freight revenue outstripped that from passengers in the ratio of 12 to 1. Even so, its passenger trains were for many years among the very best in the country. The fleet name of – Chief was widely used, having its origin in a train advertised as 'The Chief – extra fast, extra fine, and extra fare', which entered service towards the end of 1926 on the Chicago-Los Angeles route. Prior to that, the Santa Fe De Luxe had been a companion of the California Limited on the run, both of them crack trains.

Closely associated with passenger service on the Santa Fe from as early as 1876 was 'Fred Harvey' service. Harvey was a Scot who built up a chain of railway station restaurants on Santa Fe lines, prior to the advent of dining cars. He set high standards at a time when train meal stops were a prime subject for jokes. The Harvey Houses made a name for themselves, and expanded to become a big hotel group; for a time Harvey was also a dining car contractor.

History was made in 1937 when the Santa Fe placed in service the first diesel-powered all-first-class streamliner in the USA. The Super Chief was a beautifully appointed train, built by Budd, and it ran from Chicago to Los Angeles in under 40 hours. In 1938, it was joined by a second similar train, built by Pullman-Standard. Dome cars and more new equipment were added after the war, and in 1956, the fast all-coach (second class) economy train, the El Capitan, was equipped with so-called high-level coaches. Other crack trains of the Santa Fe included the Texas Chief and the Kansas Cityan. Today, under AMTRAK, service over Santa Fe rails is provided between Chicago and Los Angeles by the combined Super Chief/El Capitan (as well as by the Chief during the summer only), the Texas Chief to Houston and by three round trips daily between Los Angeles and San Diego.

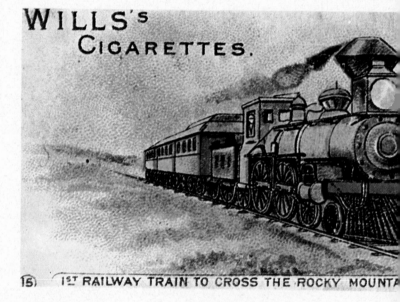

15) 1ST RAILWAY TRAIN TO CROSS THE ROCKY MOUNTA

24

Pacific type 4-6-2 locomotive of the
Oregon Short Line later absorbed in
the Union Pacific. V Goldberg collection

Atlantic-type 4-4-2 of the Oregon Short
line with a Vanderbilt tender.
V Goldberg collection

Wills cigarette card depicting early
American-type 4-4-0 wood-burning
locomotive circa 1870, labelled 'The
first railway train to cross the Rocky
Mountains'.

Diesel-hauled City of San Francisco in
Echo Canyon. Union Pacific RR

Typical Consolidation
goods engine of the Union Pacific
built in the 1890s. V Goldberg collection

UNION PACIFIC BIG BOYS

To railroad fans, the initials UP have always stood for UNION PACIFIC, but to students of mechanical engineering those same initials recall the phrase 'unlimited power', and there is no better slogan with which to describe Union Pacific motive power practice.

The Union Pacific was part of the first American transcontinental railroad. Particularly in respect of locomotive policy, its progressive management enjoyed a reputation for research, for innovation and for an ability to operate a stud of locomotives representing the ultimate in technical development and capable performance. Thus it was no accident that UP steam power was invariably ahead of the company's current requirements; that freight trains ran on schedules which were highly satisfactory to shippers; and that the combined tonnage and speeds achieved resulted in an operating ratio which even the most exacting system cost accountant termed efficient.

The Big Boys were no isolated achievement. The research and development that went into their construction came from a wealth of experience and a long line of remarkable locomotives. By 1930, the railroad had in service almost one hundred 4-12-2s designed, in the words of the then chief of motive power, 'to haul mile-long freight trains at passenger train speeds'. That their 4,330hp was capable of pulling at 50mph the same train that the Mallet compounds they replaced could only struggle with at 25mph was never in doubt.

The 4-12-2s were unique on four counts. They represented the high watermark in North America in size of locomotive with rigid frames, being the largest non-articulateds ever built. They were the only 12-coupled locomotives constructed in the States. In an age when built-up crank axles had been superseded by a straight two-cylinder design, the 9000s were given three cylinders. And finally, all but a handful were fitted with the Gresley conjugate valve gear (though I never met anyone who knew the origin of that name).

The next significant development came in 1936, when the Challenger 4-6-6-4 wheel arrangement was introduced. By then the railway had gone right away from the Mallet, or compound articulated, into the realm of simple articulated locomotives. The 3900s were not only remarkable looking engines, they were the first articulateds able to achieve mile-a-minute speeds due to improved front-end boiler support and articulated joints. Indeed, the Challenger was a true dual-purpose or mixed-traffic engine and on 'second sections' and passenger extras, speeds in the seventies have been recorded.

In parallel with the development of the 4-6-6-4s, the 800s, or Northern 4-8-4s, were introduced. At 456 short tons, they were among the heaviest locomotives of that wheel arrangement. The 4-8-4s looked good on the drawing board and were even better in steel and steam at the head end. Until the advent of the 800s, the older Mountain-class 4-8-2s had reached the limit of tonnage and speed. Double-heading was the rule and UP head-quarters in Omaha were looking for something to boost speeds, increase tonnage and cut costs. They certainly found it with the 800s. From the very start in 1937, the first 20 engines in the class averaged 15,000 miles per month per locomotive and pushed up the availability from 65.3 per cent in the case of the Mountains to a remarkable figure of 93.4 per cent.

Costwise, the 800s effected the economy required by management. During the first year of operation, savings of $1¼ million were turned in, being attributed to more-efficient operation, and the elimination of double-heading and extra sections (reliefs). The return on investment achieved was slightly over 50 per cent.

Many of the features of the 800s later came to be employed on the Big Boys. The 4-8-4s were the first locomotives on the system to be fitted with roller bearings on all axles and the first to have a boiler of 300lb pressure, which was to play such an important part in the Big Boy story. Other new features were the use of a manually controlled blow-off and sludge-removal system, needle-roller bearings for all valve motion parts and mechanical forced-feed lubrication applied widely throughout the locomotive. The 800s were designed for continuous 90mph operation and early on it was discovered that 3,000 miles could be attained between entering engine terminals for servicing. A typical 1949 diagram of that mileage would be Kansas City – Denver – La Grande – Green River – Ogden – Cheyenne, and in those days it was rare for an 800 to fail to complete its diagram.

Train X4023 (in the text) starting off downhill from Sherman after the pilot was detached.   Lord Garnock

UP Big Boy No 4012, preserved at Steamtown locomotive museum. D K Johnson

Thus was the stage set for the introduction in 1941 of the first of the Big Boys, of which 25 were to be built by Alco at Schenectady, New York, before the end of the war. The huge 4-8-8-4 simple articulateds were the brain-child of the same successful partnership that had directed UP motive power policy throughout the thirties – Jabelman and Jeffers. The former, occupied the position of chief of research and development, motive power and machinery; the latter was chief mechanical engineer.

At the close of the nineteen-thirties, the effects of the depression had ended and American industry was firmly established and expanding fast out on the west coast to escape from the over-populated eastern seaboard. Los Angeles and San Francisco, and indeed the whole of California, were expanding at a rate four-and-a-half times the national average. An ever-increasing freight traffic movement was apparent, linking the population growth in the Pacific with the traditional eastern and midwestern markets. By building heavier and more-powerful freight locomotives, the board of the Union Pacific was determined to increase the railway's share of the traffic.

Late in 1940, Otto Jabelman decided that not even the 40 Challengers would eliminate the older Mallets from double-heading and banking on the Wahsatch and Sherman grades, where the main line crosses the two toughest ranges within the Rockies. By tradition, the American Locomotive Company had built the UP's

modern power, and Alco was again consulted. This resulted in drawings being prepared under Jabelman's direction for what were the largest steam locomotives in the world, the 4-8-8-4 Big Boys. Such was their size that none ever surpassed them, so the title was retained until the scrapyard cutting torch took its toll in the early nineteen-sixties.

Previous wheel arrangements all carried distinguishing names – Mountain (4-8-2), Union Pacific (4-12-2), Northern (4-8-4) and Challenger (4-6-6-4), and a similarly stirring name was planned for the 4-8-8-4s. However, history does not relate what it was, because events overtook the decision. The first engine was universally known as *Big Boy*, and the name, originally thought to have been coined by a fitter at the Alco plant, stuck and was officially retained.

The first engine, No 4000, was handed over to the railroad at Council Bluffs on September 4, 1941, and immediately went into freight service between Cheyenne and Ogden hauling tonnage trains over the severe mountain grades. The engine arrived on the UP not without incident. Schenectady is in the eastern seaboard state of New York and never previously had anything weighing 605 short tons in working order had to be worked the 1,500 miles from there to the Union Pacific. It proved to be a slow and tedious journey.

27

One of the more delightful, though possibly apocryphal, stories of those early days with No 4000 occurred during a luncheon the Union Pacific board gave to the Chamber of Trade and business community in Omaha to celebrate the arrival of the first Big Boy, which was by then in freight service west of Cheyenne. There had always been tremendous rivalry between the railway and its competitor, the Northern Pacific, which had an equal reputation for operating large locomotives and immensely long freight trains. At that date the NP had been claiming the largest locomotive, in its Yellowstone 2-8-8-4 Class Z5 engines. The Big Boys surpassed the Yellowstones in size and weight, though not in tractive effort or grate area.

Towards the end of the luncheon the UP president rose to his feet to toast the Big Boy, concluding his speech ' . . . so I am now proudly able to say that once again the Union Pacific have the largest locomotive on earth'. His words were particularly apt, because at that moment the first Big Boy had derailed at a place where there was a low fill leaving the divisional master mechanic scratching his head as to precisely how something of that weight should be 'put back on'.

The 4000s had a wheelbase of 117ft 7in and an overall length of 132ft 9¼in, engine and tender. This extreme length necessitated installing 136ft turntables in the roundhouses at Cheyenne, Green River, Laramie and Ogden, all terminals on the main line to the Pacific coast. At other places the engines were 'wyed', while at one or two terminals with only a standard length table the engines were 'jack-knifed'. This was a remarkable process in which the engine was run forward over and past the end of the table to enable lifting frogs to be placed behind the tender wheels. The engine was then backed on to the table, with the rear wheels of the tender elevated enough off the end to allow the table to rotate.

All 25 Big Boys were put into pool service between Cheyenne in the east and Ogden in the west, representing the mountain divisions of the UP main line. The Union Pacific divides into two distinct parts. At the eastern end the railroad starts at Council Bluffs, Iowa/Omaha, Nebraska (two cities facing one another across the Missouri river) and runs for 528 miles across the rolling prairies of Nebraska to Cheyenne in the extreme south-east corner of Wyoming. In that distance, the track, and indeed the whole terrain, gradually climbs at ten feet each mile uniformly, which averages 1 in 500 for 500 miles without a steep ruling grade. Thus Cheyenne, the capital of Wyoming, is reached at an altitude of 6,060 feet above sea level before the Union Pacific starts mountain railroading. Needless to say, Big Boys were never to be found on the Nebraska division, nor indeed east of Cheyenne.

Westward out of Cheyenne, before the so-called new line was built in the 1950s 'to ease the grades and help the diesels', the first 31 miles required westbound trains to be lifted 1,953 feet, to an elevation of 8,013 feet at Sherman summit, on a ruling grade of 1 in 64½ and an average of 1 in 85. The distance over the Wyoming and Utah divisions from Cheyenne to Ogden is somewhat less than so-called level railroading across Nebraska, but it includes the two rugged climbs over Sherman and, west of Green river, through the Wahsatch range with a ruling grade of 1 in 88. The Wahsatch grade was the principal factor in the decision made at an early stage in the design of the 4-8-8-4s that maximum continuous horsepower output should take place at 30mph.

The Big Boys were not often noted in passenger service, although they were designed for speeds of up to 70mph. During the war they were known on troop trains and in the mid-1940s an occasional passenger extra felt their tremendous force but they were rare birds to be seen heading a 'string of varnish'. On freights they excelled.

While most aspects of railroading in North America are large in the widest sense of the word, nonetheless, one was still not quite prepared for the sheer size and bulk of a Big Boy. In the States, mechanical dimensions tend to be given in small units such as pounds and inches — possibly to make the resultant large figures larger still, or more probably because most formulae and calculation require that form — with an impressive result in the case of the 4000s. The locomotive alone weighed 772,000lb and the total with tender in working order was 1,209,000lb. The sheet length of 132ft 9¼in carried on 16 68in drivers and two four-wheel trucks (all fitted with roller bearings) gave the effect of a giant centipede from the age of the dinosaur.

Above: Prototype three-cylinder 4-12-2 No 9000, forerunner of a class total of 102 engines. Union Pacific RR

Below: 4000-class Big Boy 4-8-8-4 No 4019 climbing Weber canyon, Utah, with an extra (X in the train number) freight train of refrigerated wagons. Union Pacific RR

Above: UP 2-8-8-2 No 3525 climbing a 1 in 50 grade in the Blue mountains with a 75-car train, and No 3613 banking. R H Kindig

The four cylinders, admittedly not as impressive in size as their low-pressure counterparts on a true Mallet, but still eyecatching at 23¾in bore and a 32in stroke, were fed by a boiler pressed for 300lb to give a tractive effort of 135,375lb. Perhaps the most awe-inspiring statistic was to discover that the two sand boxes astride the boiler had a total capacity of three tons.

The 14-wheel centipede-type tender was no less impressive. The centipede was a development of the cylindrical Vanderbilt tank and was designed to overcome the 60,000lb axle weight restriction by using 10 rigid wheels preceded by a four-wheel truck (known as a 4-10-0 tender arrangement). The 42in wheels were all mounted on roller bearings. Capacities varied slightly on the different marks of centipede tank, but the final arrangement for the tenders running behind Nos 4020-24 took 25,000 US gallons of water and 28 short tons of coal. Additional baffle plates were fitted after early experience of surging, particularly when the water

was down to half capacity or less. Cheyenne yard and terminal used to abound in stories of head-end brakesmen and firemen arriving back off Sherman hill ashenfaced from what became known as 'centipede sickness'. In common with US practice, the tender contained a worm-wheel stoker.

At one stage in design of the locomotive, boosters were considered, but they were not used. The boiler varied in diameter between 95in and 105in, with a welded firebox 235in by 96½in, and a combustion chamber 112in in length. It is wonderful what can be done with a loading gauge of 15ft 6in height and 10ft 9in width and an axle load of 30 short tons running on 133lb rail! In accordance with normal UP practice at that date, a live-steam injector was fitted on one side and an exhaust-steam and centrifugal pumps on the other. The locomotive was given a double chimney consisting of four-jet exhaust nozzles on a common base.

Experiments in oil-firing were carried out on No 4005

This page top: Picture from the fireman's seat
of a Big Boy being piloted up the 1 in 69
Sherman grade by a 4-6-6-4 Challenger.
Lord Garnock

Above: Cheyenne (Wyoming) roundhouse, with
46 stalls and 136ft turntable, and engine
repair shops in background. Lord Garnock

Left: One of the first of the 4000-class
shortly after delivery to UP from Alco.
Union Pacific RR

during 1947-48, but the single burner could not get the fire close enough to the crown to generate the required heat. The resultant poor oil combustion necessitated reconversion back to coal in March 1948.

The two engine beds on the 4-8-8-4s were connected by means of a vertical articulated hinge, so arranged that when the boiler was full, a seven-ton load was applied to the tongue of the rear bed unit; consequently, the two engine beds were held rigid in the vertical plane, unlike what had been experienced with their predecessors. A new type of articulated side rod was fitted to eliminate the more-usual knuckle-pin connections. Each set of cylinders and frame was produced in an integral mono-block casting. The live and exhaust steam pipes were larger than anything previously used to permit better utilisation of boiler capacity and obtain maximum power output.

One of the more novel – for 1941 – innovations was the running gear arrangement, in which a system of lateral motion control was designed to fit all wheels to the rails thus to reduce binding on curvature to a minimum. In addition, it adjusted the wheels to vertical track differential with minimum disturbance to the weight distribution of the locomotive. The effect was to produce a stable engine on straight track but with the ability to adjust to curvature. Consequently the Big Boys used to 'heel to the curves' smoothly without the tell-tale violent front-end oscillation or nosing so characteristic of articulateds. From the cab, the impression on curves was totally different from riding on articulateds of other railroads. On the latter in a curve, this writer used to be left with the feeling of the front drivers answering to the curvature while the boiler (rigid to the rear drivers) continued straight on for what seemed an age before suddenly jerking round when the rear drivers hit the curve.

The punishment to which the Big Boys were subjected was considerable, so that a word or two on their performance will not be out of place. One hot July day in 1949, westbound extra freight consisting of ninety-nine loads and seven empties plus caboose (107 cars weighing 5,192 tons) was awaiting the 'high ball' to leave Cheyenne yard behind 4-8-8-4 No 4023 (I was on the footplate), with 4-6-6-4 No 3819 as pilot. One moment the two giants were quietly simmering in the heat, and the next, a roar like thunder as the engineers opened their throttles and prepared to surmount the 1 in 81 grade immediately they emerged on to the main line.

Engineer Hooker of the Big Boy started by using 65 per cent cut-off and full throttle, but after four miles, in which speed had reached 19mph, there came the ruling grade of 1 in 64½; even though the cut-off was altered to 75 per cent, speed gradually dropped in five miles to 8mph. Another two miles and speed had increased by one mile per hour, but only at the expense of the boiler pressure which had declined (small wonder with full throttle and 75 per cent cut-off) from 295 to 260lb; so, the Elesco pump was temporarily shut off until the pressure increased. By that time all normal sounds were eliminated by the pounding and slipping of 28 driving-wheels; the sun was entirely blotted out by the combined efforts of both exhausts and a black mass resembling a thunder cloud drifted in the otherwise clear atmosphere right the way back to Cheyenne.

The 'extra freight west' restarted 12½ minutes after arriving there and achieved 14mph in six minutes nine seconds, when the 4-6-6-4 pusher dropped off. Speed thereupon began to diminish and was down to 5mph when the grade changed for the better to 1 in 81. I thought that No 4023 would be given some respite there, but still Hooker kept his engine at full throttle and in full forward gear. Back to 5mph for some more ruling grade, but on the final six miles of lighter grades, we hit 16mph for the first time in two hours eleven minutes, and when the train stopped at Sherman to detach the pilot, the 31 miles had taken 162¼ minutes running time. Throughout, the Big Boy had been worked at full throttle and never less than 65 per cent cut-off, spending 109 minutes in full forward gear! It had used about 23 tons of coal and 26,000 gallons of water in 31 miles, all in order to lift 5,000 tons a vertical height of 2,000 feet.

The description of that particular run has been included to illustrate the way in which the 4000s could be operated under arduous conditions. It is not typical of Sherman in that our pilot, No 3819, was not steaming well and therefore contributing less than would normally have been expected.

The Big Boys truly lived up to their name and reputation. Perhaps the most memorable sight of all was the view forward from the cab of a 4-8-8-4 piloted by a 4-6-6-4. The tender of the pilot engine seemed far enough away, but the whole combination appeared to stretch far into the distance . . .

Otto water-tower hove into sight and when we stopped with our pilot spotted opposite the column we were 69¾ minutes and 14 miles out of Cheyenne. To save restarting the train twice, the second engine is watered by cutting the locomotives off the train and running them forward. But to start the train once, let alone twice, required considerable ingenuity, as it is impossible for a train of that tonnage to be restarted on a 1 in 64½ grade by only two locomotives. The regular procedure is that a freight train stopped at the water tower is banked by the pilot engine of the following freighter, the pusher dropping off when it comes up to the water-column — thus each train has rear-end assistance for restarting. Freight trains are sent 'over the top' in batches of about four or five during lulls in the passenger service; the fifth or last train is lightly loaded so that it can get away from Otto without rear-end assistance.

Top: Another view of No 4012 at Steamtown. D K Johnson

Centre: Line-up of UP's big steam power at Cheyenne engine house in 1949, with two Big Boys on the nearest track, two Class 800 4-8-4s next, and two Class 3900 engines at extreme right. Lord Garnock

Bottom: A typical Mallet, a Denver & Rio Grande Western 2-8-8-2, climbing 1 in 33 Tennessee pass, Colorado, at 15mph with a passenger train in 1949, illustrating how the front drivers 'heel' into the curve before the boiler starts to deviate. Lord Garnock

CAMELBACKS & MOTHER HUBBARDS

In days of steam traction, whenever one lit upon a locomotive of bizarre or unusual appearance one could be reasonably sure that fuel was at the bottom of it. Examples near our own time included the Crostis of British Railways and Italian State Railways, and the Bulleid turf-burner of Coras lompair Eireann; but none became such a widespread cult, and an effective cult, as the Wootten-firebox engines beginning in 1877 and lasting until after the 1939-45 war.

The exceptionally wide firebox, which usually had to go above coupled wheels, meant there was insufficient space for a cab in the normal location; so a special cab was made to go over the boiler barrel and the driver was ensconced on one side of it. The fireman was kept at the back end, and rarely was he given more than the scantiest protection.

Such engines, use of which was almost wholly (perhaps 99 per cent) confined to the USA, were from early days colloquially known as camelbacks or Mother Hubbards; there were even times when they were referred to as such in the staid reports of the Interstate Commerce Commission. Mother Hubbard arose from the large windowed cupboard appearance of the wooden cab astride the boiler; camelback arose similarly from the hump-like contour of the locomotive's side elevation. The reason for the ungainly arrangement was anthracite fuel, and the type appeared first on just those railroads which from around 1840 had been using anthracite for their locomotives. From 1840· to 1850, the early

examples had been known as camels, and were associated particularly with the builder Ross Winans. They had a fairly narrow firebox entirely behind the rear pair of wheels — a long-boiler type, in fact.

There was one big difference. The camels used top-quality anthracite and big firebox volume was not essential for such fuel; but a larger grate than usual was desirable and that could be obtained with a long narrow grate as easily as with extra width. With just one or two exceptions, the long-grate type was perpetuated until the mid-1870s on those roads serving the large anthracite beds. Winan's own engines often had fireboxes of remarkable shape, not unlike some of Crampton's efforts in England.

A feature of the anthracite industry as a whole was that the handling and preparation of the friable fuel resulted in an immense amount of dust (culm), reckoned at times to represent 18 or 20 per cent of the whole production. It was gathered into enormous heaps at any convenient place near the breakers, and left, for it was too fine for domestic use or general industrial purposes. It was to make use of the huge quantities of culm that John E Wootten evolved his patent firebox, for as the culm could be had almost for the asking, he foresaw a big reduction in his railroad's fuel bill if he could use it without running into consequential troubles. His success was evidenced by a reduction of $380,000 a year in the coal purchases of the Philadelphia & Reading road when 170 to 200 Wootten-box locomotives were in service in 1884.

A wide firebox does not make a Wootten. Ivatt's big-boilered Atlantics on the Great Northern Railway in England were often referred to as Wootten types, but they were not. The Wootten box was an extremely wide and exceptionally shallow structure designed specifically to burn culm, or buckwheat anthracite as it was sometimes called. As such, it had a very large grate to give the low firing rate needed with dust, and the small firebox volume that is sufficient for the short flame of anthracite. To suit the thin but very hot bed of fire the grate bars were nearly always in the form of water tubes.

So shallow were the earlier boxes that the top of the coal bed could be level with the bottom row of tubes; and common practice was to put a low brick wall across the front of the grate, so that even with comparatively high firing rates, the dust would not be carried straight through the tubes. This arrangement, and a combustion chamber, were parts of Wootten's master patent of 1877; but a later patent catered even for boxes wherein the grate bars were a few inches *above* the bottom tubes — to suit engines with larger wheels than those of the normal freight engine of the time and yet retain a low boiler pitch.

However, such nice considerations of space were alleviated as soon as it was realised that a low locomotive centre of gravity was no longer essential, and that boiler pitch could be raised appreciably. Credit for achieving the change of design in North America is usually given to Theo N Ely, of the Pennsylvania Railroad, in his bituminous coal-burning K-class 4-4-0s of 1844. Actually, Wootten was the first to introduce the practice when he went to 7ft 8in pitch in 1880, 2in more than Ely's figure of four years later.

This heightening of boiler pitch solved the teething troubles with the Wootten boilers of 1877-79. Also it enabled a flat grate to be used instead of the slight slope of the early boxes; and the combustion chamber was shortened or almost eliminated, thereby reducing construction costs. Further, the higher pitch widened the possible applications to 4-4-0s from 1880; previously the box had been confined to small-wheel freight and mineral 4-6-0s.

Absence of teething troubles on any scale was due much to the audacity with which Wootten, as general manager of the Philadelphia & Reading, tackled the whole business. Previously he had for five years been superintendent of motive power of the road, and he realised fully that large grate area was essential to give the slow combustion rate needed. But not many men in a position where they had to bear full responsibility would have gone from the 18sq ft of large American--type 4-4-0s at one bound to 64sq ft, and within three years to have gone up to 76sq ft. Provision of such a grate naturally changed locomotive appearance considerably, and introduced some problems of weight distribution. In those days, the very weight of the box itself was more than could be supported on a single trailing carrying axle; but in any case such wheel arrangements had not really arrived in 1877-80, even for normal boiler locomotives.

From 1880 Wootten-box engines went straight into the main-line class; in the previous three years the 25 or so locomotives fitted had been slow-speed freight and mineral haulers with six-coupled wheels; and the still older camels had been mainly 0-8-0s. The P & R 4-4-0s of 1880-84 were far larger than any others in the US at that time, and had cylinders of 20 and 21in bore, usually with a short 22in stroke, a pressure of 140lb, a firebox heating surface of 130 to 150sq ft out of an evaporative total of 1,100 to 1,200sq ft, a grate area of 65 to 76sq ft, and a weight of 47 to 50 tons. Wheels were 60 to 65in, the firebox was wholly above them, and the enormous ashpan, with hand-operated hopper doors at the bottom, was wholly between the frames, for triple-section pans were out of the question with the revolving side rods.

Above: Artist's impression of typical
camelback engine having a Wootten firebox
with enormous grate area to burn inferior fuel.
P F Winding

Lehigh & Hudson River Railway
2-8-0 No 58 pictured at Maybrook, New York,
in May 1933. W Monypeny (C T Andrews)

Following the almost universal practice with wood-burning American-type 4-4-0s, the blast nozzle was adjustable from the cab, and set low down in the smokebox, often level with the bottom row of tubes. Centralised coupled-axlebox lubrication from a single oil box began with these engines. Although inside Stephenson motion operating outside slide valves through cross shafts was common, the first use of Joy radial motion in the USA was on one of these P & R 4-4-0s in 1882 — and in his diary Joy recorded how the engine rocked and rolled at bad places, and what an almighty slam the weight of the big firebox at the back end produced when going over a soft spot at a mile a minute.

The curious position of the cab was not a feature of the earliest Woottens; in fact it had a European origin. Wootten sent a 4-6-0 to a Paris exhibition of 1878, and at the closure one or two trial runs over the French Nord and Est systems were proposed. The loading gauge would not pass the cab as it was originally, spread out over the firebox, in which engineer and fireman were together. Therefore a cab was fabricated in France to go over the barrel, and the driver transferred thither. From 1879 Wootten adopted the same practice in the USA, as it solved in advance difficulties of growing boiler and firebox sizes, even within the generous American loading gauge.

Separation of the driver and fireman was not a principle accepted readily by leading railroads, even though there was a side platform or walkway connection between the two, and an occasional installation of a speaking tube. The Pennsylvania did try camelbacks once, on the first three Atlantics it ever possessed; but higher management vetoed the idea of a separated crew within a matter of weeks, and the engines were transferred to the subsidiary Long Island Railroad. The Pennsy, however, was a bituminous coal road, and had

no real economic use for Wootten fireboxes. The anthracite roads, such as the P & R, Lehigh Valley, Lackawanna, Delaware & Hudson, and Central of New Jersey, took up the idea for both freight and passenger power; but with a few exceptions their trains did not run at high speeds.

One important exception was the Camden-Atlantic City fliers of the P & R, and for those trains, Wottenbox single-drivers, 2-4-2s and then Atlantics, were developed; it was to compete with the speeds put up by the last-named that the Pennsylvania first went to the 4-4-2. The Reading's (P & R's) first 4-2-2 ran only trial trips in 1880, and then was taken back by Baldwin, as the Reading was in poor financial shape at the time and the builder feared for his money.

This action led directly to the only Wootten-firebox locomotive to run in England; after standing a few weeks in Baldwin's shop the ex-P & R No 507 was bought by the Eames Brake Company and shipped to Liverpool to take part in continuous-brake trials on the Lancashire & Yorkshire Railway. After trials in 1881-82, and exhibition at Alexandra Palace, the *Lovett Eames,* as the engine was named, stood in a shed at Wood Green on the GNR, and was sold for scrap in 1884; but its brass bell was used at Kings Cross locomotive shed and then at the newer Hornsey depot for many years.

The cab had to be contracted to fall within the English loading gauge, but it was at the back end straddling the firebox, and housed both engine driver and fireman together. Thus it was not a true Mother Hubbard. But it did have the first 4,000-gallon tender in Britain; and no larger grate area was ever stoked in the British Isles than the 56sq ft of that single-driver, which was only equalled 40 years later in the LNER Beyer-Garratt. How an English fireman coped with 56sq ft and a low box with bituminous coal has not been recorded,

but probably a big section of the grate was blocked off with firebrick or a cast-iron plate.

With *Lovett Eames* as first built for the P & R was initiated the practice of spreading the Wootten box out over trailing carrying wheels, which were highly loaded. It led, also, to two further single-drivers for the P & R, rare birds for the USA, and even rarer here for they were of Vauclain compound type; but a few years after their construction in 1895 they were converted to two-cylinder simple-expansion 4-4-0s.

The Reading's P-class Wootten-box Atlantics, with 84in and 86in wheels, gained a reputation for speed on the Atlantic City route, running the 55½ miles non-stop at first in 60 minutes, and then to accelerated timings, until one special run was timed at 46½ minutes, or 71.6 mph start-to-stop. The Reading's final camelback passenger development was a 4-4-4 with a grate area of 108sq ft, but the four engines of 1914-15 were converted to 4-4-2 after a year or two.

Mother Hubbards of 4-4-0, 4-6-0 and 4-8-0 arrangement were favourites for passenger and freight traffic, and the Lehigh Valley's crack passenger train, the Black Diamond, ran between Jersey City and Buffalo for years behind Wootten-box 4-4-0s with 80in wheels. There were a number of three-cylinder camelbacks, a few of which had two sets of valve gear conjugated on Gresley's system. At least 16 different wheel arrangements were known, varying from single drivers to decapods, plus one class of three 0-8-8-0 Mallet compounds on the Erie. Only one tank engine type was known − a 2-6-6T. About 40 different railroads used camelbacks at one time or another, some of them having only a single example. About 95 per cent of the total number of camelbacks were on the eastern roads running through or touching the big anthracite deposits; odd men out included the Southern Pacific, Union Pacific, and Canadian Pacific, with no more than a handful each.

Firing a camelback was a unique process. It was done more or less out in the open, on the front of a bucketing tender, with only a couple of side chains as protection against a fall-off and rarely more than a curved plate above − and often not even with that. There were two fireholes, so the fuel could be got into the back corners of a box 8ft to 9ft wide. Not often did one man have to shovel more than 3,000lb an hour, but shovelling culm was not always so easy as firing the same amount of bituminous coal; great skill was needed to keep a thin even fire free from holes over a box 8ft to 9ft wide and 9ft to 12 ft long.

Culm could not be handled by mechanical stoking devices as they were up to the early 1920s. After that, they were hardly considered, for from 1918 the Interstate Commerce Commission banned further new construction of Mother Hubbards. Separation of the crew was not favoured by unions or railroads; the driver's position was almost hopeless if a side rod broke at speed, and so the number of camelbacks in traffic slowly decreased.

However, the last engines did not disappear from regular service until 1954, though from the end of the 1939-45 war, when there were still over 50 in traffic, the only road operating them normally was the Central of New Jersey, which used its 4-6-0s with 90sq ft of grate area on local passenger trains until the end. One of them, No 592 built in 1901, is preserved in Baltimore; a Lackawanna 4-4-0 is on exhibition in St Louis; and a small 0-4-0 that began life on the Reading and was subsequently in industry, is preserved on the Strasbourg Railway in Pennsylvania, though last reports are that it is no longer in working order.

Left: Lehigh & Hudson River Railway
4-6-0s at Warwick, New York, in April 1919.
W Monypeny (C T Andrews)

Below: Lehigh Valley 4-4-0 on exhibition
heading the Black Diamond express at Easton,
Pa, in May 1896 just before its first run.
C T Andrews

SOME GIANTS OF STEAM

There are various reasons why American railway loco-motives grew to such staggering proportions. One is the enormous length of freight trains, and consequently the prodigious loads which the engines were expected to haul. Whereas in Europe or Japan a freight train of 2,000 tons would be regarded as exceptional, 10,000 and upwards is by no means uncommon in the United States. Indeed, the heaviest regular train loads in the world were the responsibility of the Duluth, Missabes & Iron Range RR, which company used massive 2-8-8-4 Mallet engines weighing 508 tons to work iron ore trains at 30mph — and these mammoth trains loaded to an incredible 12,550 to 15,550 tons.

For many years, the American Brotherhood had dictated the size of train crews, and it was clearly to the advantage of the railroads to economise by reducing the number of trains — and consequently, to increase the length of individual trains to the absolute maximum. Another aspect of railway operation which has made it necessary to provide such ample motive power, is the terrain traversed by some companies' lines. This applies particularly to routes which reach the Pacific coast via tortuous crossings of the Rocky Mountains. The main line of the Union Pacific, for example, on its way from Omaha to Los Angeles and San Francisco, has to climb to a summit of 8,013ft near Cheyenne. The Santa Fe is no better off, and its switchback road from Chicago to Los Angeles has to negotiate gradients of 1 in 28½ for long stretches in the mountain section. Farther south, in Colorado, we find the Denver & Rio Grande Western RR slogging up to the breathless height of 10,239ft at its summit in the Tennessee pass. To surmount natural obstacles of this order was no picnic for any form of traction, and it is small wonder that some mammoth steam power was called for.

North America as a whole was a very early entrant into the diesel age, and made such rapid progress with the new form of traction that by the mid nineteen-fifties steam had been eclipsed almost completely. For all the pictures and tabulated details, nobody who did not have the good fortune to cross the Atlantic during their halcyon years, can have any real conception of the gigantic proportions to which the North American steam locomotive finally grew. But in order properly to appreciate its development, it is necessary that we should make a journey backwards in time, to the early years of the present century, for it was then that the American 'big engine' was reaching its adolescence.

In 1910 the American Locomotive Company (ALCO) produced a prototype 4-6-2 express passenger engine which was a considerable success, and was destined to have a profound influence not only over the future of American express engine development, but in the progress of subsequent European designs as well. The ALCO locomotive was the forerunner of the famous K4 Pacifics of the Pennsylvania RR, about 425 of which were constructed between 1914 and 1927. These handsome engines were responsible for hauling the Pennsylvania's principal express trains until well after the United States entered the Second World War, and some survived until the late 'fifties.

The K4s had 6ft 8in driving wheels, a boiler pressure of 205lb per sq in, a tractive effort of 39,300lb, a grate area of 70sq ft and a total weight in working order of nearly 225 tons.

In due course, as American express trains became faster and heavier, the 4-6-2 (Pacific) type was super-seded by the 4-6-4 (Baltic), the most remarkable examples being the New York Central RR Hudsons. From their introduction in 1927, these 297-tonners began to make a name for themselves in the realm of heavy high-speed haulage. Heading 1,000-ton trains at 75mph along level track for long distances was a commonplace feat for them. The New York Central possessed 275 of these fine engines, in a number of varieties — some were streamlined — but all were provided with 'boosters' on the trailing wheels, a sort of supplementary engine which raised the starting tractive effort in the later versions to 55,540lb or nearly 25 tons.

The Hudsons became a legend for their work on such trains as the Empire State Express and the Twentieth Century Limited, the latter involving through working from Harmon, outside New York (where steam took over from electric traction) to Chicago, a distance of 925 miles. The Twentieth Century Limited loaded up to 1,000 tons and the 958-mile journey was booked for an average speed of almost exactly 60mph, inclusive of seven stops. The Hudsons have been credited with speed achievements in the region of 125mph.

Perhaps predictably, the final generation of North American steam passenger engines took the form of a 4-8-4. First in the field was the Northern Pacific RR, which introduced such a wheel arrangement in 1926. Not surprisingly, they called the type the Northern, but the name did not stick, and on other railroads the 4-8-4 type was variously dubbed Niagara, Dixie, Daylight, Wyoming, Greenbrier and Pocono. The Daylights belong-ed to the Southern Pacific RR, and a magnificent sight they made, clad in distinctive red, orange and black livery hauling the famous Daylight Expresses.

Farther north, in Canada, the 4-8-4 also found favour for fast heavy mainline passenger work, culminating in 1927-8 in the 6100 class of the Canadian National Railway. At a total weight with tender of 285 tons, they were the largest steam passenger engines ever to run in the Dominion. It is pleasing to note that CNR No 6218, built in 1942 as a smaller version of the same general type, has been retained in active service by the Canadian National for use on enthusiasts' special trains, and provided money can be raised privately (about $250,000) for essential repairs for which Canadian National is not prepared to pay, it is probable that the awe-inspiring spectacle of a really large steam locomotive hauling an express passenger train will be possible for some years yet.

It is, of course, in the realm of heavy freight haulage that most of the records for sheer size and power were broken. It was appreciated many years ago that there

Top: Union Pacific
Railroad's 4-8-4 No 8444.
P B Whitehouse

Bottom: A Canadian
National Railways 4-8-4
No 6218, the last loco-
motive to work in steam
in Canada in the late
1960s. P B Whitehouse

Top: Lima-built 2-8-4 No 759 for the Nickel
Plate Road in the 1940s, pictured in steam at
Hagastown in 1970. P B Whitehouse

Right: Canadian Pacific No 2816, a Hudson
4-6-4, sadly out to grass at Steam Town,
Vermont P B Whitehouse

was a limit to the power that could be obtained from a conventional rigid-framed steam locomotive. Admittedly the Southern Pacific Daylight 4-8-4s, with boosters on their trailing wheels, could muster the incredible tractive force of 78,660lb. The Pennsylvania RR built some fine streamliners in 1945-6 with the most unusual wheel arrangement of 4-4-4-4. In effect, they were 4-8-4s with the driving mechanism divided into two groups, giving the advantage of lighter revolving parts at the expense of a slightly longer wheelbase. These T1s were designed to give the output of two K4 Pacifics without recourse to articulation, and they proved capable of reaching 100mph with trains of upwards of 1,000 tons, producing more than 6,100hp. In the matter of coupled axles, for fast freight haulage, the Union Pacific had got as far as six with its 9000-class 4-12-2 three-cylinder engines of 1926. These locomotives, of which 88 were built by ALCO, could manage 3,800-ton train loads at 35mph comfortably on gradients of 1 in 122.

But that was the height of achievement of rigid frames, and articulation made possible the development of considerably greater power on a more flexible engine wheelbase, so that the Mallet system came to be generally adopted by the US railroads. Put simply, the principle of Mallet articulation is the provision of two independently driven engine units, the rear one being fixed rigidly to the locomotive frame, while the forward unit is hinged to it and free to swing laterally. Independent cylinders are provided to power the two units, which both carry a proportion of the locomotive's weight. Anatole Mallet, the French originator, began advocating the use of articulated locomotives as long ago as 1884, claiming for them (among other advantages) that the division of the driving mechanism would reduce the tendency towards violent slipping. Most of the US Mallets were built as compounds (ie steam driving both high- and low-pressure cylinders) but in time this became impracticable as low pressure cylinders grew to impossible proportions, although the Norfolk & Western RR persisted with compounding until 1952.

First in the field with articulated designs was the Baltimore & Ohio, whose 1904 ALCO-built Mallet was the largest locomotive in the world at that time. In 1911 the Santa Fe rebuilt two 2-10-2 engines into a single 2-10-10-2 weighing no less than 380 tons. In terms of bulk, the 'old' type of compound Mallet reached an acme with the Virginian RR's 400-ton 2-10-10-2 of 1918. Although intended principally for pushing one of these immense machines is reported to have hauled a train of 17,000 tons.

In 1912 the Southern Pacific RR came along with its highly distinctive 'cab forward' 2-8-8-2 Mallets, a design which was repeated with alterations until 1944, by which time the final 4-8-8-2 locomotives weighed 459 tons and produced a tractive effort of 123,000lb. It needs little imagination to see why the Southern Pacific opted for this unusual 'cab forward' arrangement — its route is exceptionally steeply graded, the ruling gradient over the 140-mile Sierra Nevada section being 1 in 41, and involved negotiating numerous tunnels. With the cab in the normal position to the rear of the chimney, the plight of the engine crew while slogging at low speed up merciless gradients through lengthy tunnels enveloped by clouds of dense black smoke, can well be imagined!

Incidentally, the Southern Pacific, single-handed the heaviest 16-car transcontinental expresses, but three were needed on the 4,000-ton 100-refrigerator-car trains. 'Smoke-splitters' were fitted to their chimneys, to prevent the savage blast from the monsters from wrecking bridges and tunnel roofs.

Not to be outdone, the Chesapeake & Ohio introduced in 1941 the heaviest engine so far — a massive 528-ton 2-6-6-6, the first time six trailing wheels had been used. The C & O also reached the ultimate extreme in boiler dimensions with its H8, the 60 examples of which could be found at the head of 160-vehicle trains no less than $1\frac{1}{3}$ miles long, slogging along at 45mph across the largest bituminous coalfield in the world. Small wonder that the engine crew could travel, across difficult terrain, for many miles without ever seeing the caboose (guard's van) at the rear, and communication was, of necessity, by radio.

In order to cope in the marshalling yards with the trains that these vast engines could haul, shunting engines (switchers) acquired proportionately alarming dimensions, the absolute extreme being reached with the Duluth RR 0-10-2s of 1936. Similarly, engine tenders were massive things to cater for the insatiable appetites of their masters. With firegrate areas of 70sq ft (the Pennsylvania K4s), 108sq ft (Union Pacific 4-12-2s) and 139sq ft (Chesapeake 2-6-6-6s), manual firing had obviously become out of the question, and engines which were not oil-fired had mechanical stokers (as was required anyway, under American law, for any engine with a grate area exceeding 50sq ft). The tenders of the Pennsylvania T1 4-4-4-4's were carried on 16 wheels and weighed 193 tons, more than any British locomotive and tender combined.

It is the final development of the articulated steam engine in the hands of the Union Pacific RR that fairly takes the breath away. The Challenger class of 1936 was a simple expansion 4-6-6-4 Mallet, built to augment the 4-12-2s on the Wyoming lines. Attention had been paid to their riding qualities, and with their 5ft 9in driving wheels, the Mallet type now became suitable for 60mph running. Five years later, of course, the limit in terms of steam locomotive size and power was reached with the same company's Big Boy 4-8-8-4. These colossal machines weighed 540 tons. One wonders what Anatole Mallet (1837-1919) would have said, had he been able to see the vast proportions to which his invention eventually grew. Fortunately, more than one Big Boy is preserved — but museum pieces are no substitute for the sight of these gigantic engines, with their cowcatchers and powerful electric headlights, blackening the sky over the mountains of Wyoming at the head of a fast freight train. No gramophone record (of which there are several) can do justice to the splendour of the exhaust created by these steam giants, like a series of muffled explosions, as they strove to get a long train on the move.

Now it is replaced by the dull rumble of the diesel. No longer do restrictions of loading gauge hinder the development of power, as any number of diesel locomotive units can be coupled together and their effort co-ordinated under automatic control of one crew. The greatest era of steam railroading in the North American continent is gone.

41

The Ford Model T automobile and the 4-4-0 steam locomotive in North America have fair claims to be considered in the same category. Both became institutions of American life; both spread over the borders and over seas; both became an outer symbol of the USA; and both were built in enormous numbers. The difference was that Model T came mainly from the brain and will of one man, and was built in mass production to interchangeable limits; the 'American-type' 4-4-0 was before the time of limits-and-fits, and although to one general type, it was of infinite variety. Cheapness was an essential of each; so far as the locomotive was concerned, it was 20-22 per cent less in first cost than English machines of the same output and period.

Evolution was through a painful stage of nearly two decades, for only slowly and by many hands was the first 4-4-0 of 1836 wrought into the classic form by the early 1850s. That form was a beautifully proportioned long-wheelbase long-truck type with horizontal outside cylinders centred above the front truck, Stephenson link motion, three-point suspension, and a deep round-top firebox dropped between the coupled axles.

It came finally from the efforts of an American builder, Thomas Rogers, and his English-born technical chief, William S Hudson, and the first examples were turned out of the Rogers works at Paterson, NJ, in 1851. By 1855-56 practically every North American builder — and there were three dozen of them at that time was building nothing else for passenger and mixed working, and little other than the same design extended into a 4-6-0 for freight or steep-grade haulage; the four-coupled outnumbered the latter by at least eight to one.

Gone were all the old close-coupled short-base bogie types with loco wheelbase of 10 to 12ft, steeply inclined outside cylinders bolted to the smokebox, and haycock or vertical fireboxes, such as the Norris and Baldwin builds, which had grown directly from the popular 4-2-0 layout. The 'New England' type, with inside cylinders and short-base truck far forward, had also disappeared from the new lists; as had the few odd types with rear-axle drive like the *Gowan and Marx* and its brother — the only two steam locomotives ever to be named after bankers. They went out with the decided developments in general practice and design that began in the late 1840s, and with the progress in shop tooling. Only a handful of small makers, such as Moore & Richardson of Cincinatti, continued the short-base truck type into the mid-1850s.

The perfected design of Rogers came just at the right time, for the route mileage open in the United States exactly doubled between 1851 and the end of 1855 — from 10,880 to 21,450 miles. In the same period, too, the number of active locomotive builders doubled, and the great majority took the Rogers basic design and proportions. Half of the builders went out of business, or out of the locomotive trade, in 1857-58 as a result of the financial panic of the former year; but the loco type remained, and its construction was carried on until the early 1880s, by which time the 4-4-0 was growing so large, so heavy and so sophisticated that no longer could it be called the American-type.

For close on half a century about 60 per cent of all locomotives running in the States and in Canada were true American-type 4-4-0s, and in the time of the

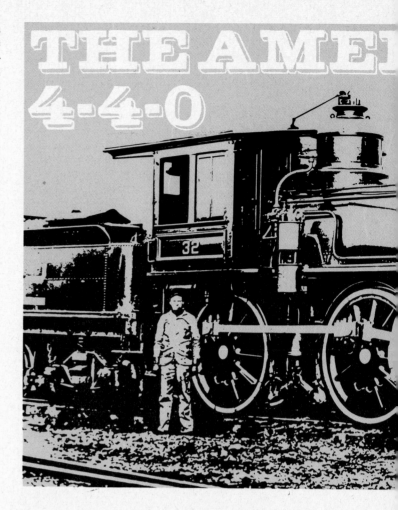

THE AMER 4-4-0

RICAN

American civil war and the decade thereafter the proportion was 80 per cent or more. Laid down in basic dimensions and wheelbase, the range was small, as it also was in certain fundamental features of construction; but the variety in appearance and embellishment was immense, and the American motive power scene was colourful and overflowing with interest. By no means were all locomotives of standard gauge. Of the 350 different roads in the US at the time of the war, 14 were laid to 6ft gauge and 125 were between 4ft 9¼in and 5ft 6in; the remaining 210 to standard gauge accounted for only 54 per cent of the total mileage, though probably for 60 per cent of the locomotive stock.

The cloud no bigger than a man's hand that presaged the disappearance, leaving, by the time of the 1914-18 war, scarcely a wrack behind, was the small-scale standardisation introduced by the Pennsylvania Railroad in 1868, for although three classes of 4-4-0 with common constituents formed the first move, they were simplified and devoid of decoration; in consequence they gradually accumulated dirt, a thing tolerated on no road in days when drivers and firemen would spend half their Sunday in cleaning up their own engine, resetting the brasses, and cutting the fat off their Sunday joint to mix with the valve oil. At about the same time the Vanderbilt lines, that later became the New York Central, pooled the locomotives so that no crew had its own engine.

It was also the Pennsylvania that took the lead in another great departure that edged the true American type of history and cinema into the conventional 4-4-0 of later years — the substitution of coal fuel for wood. That, of course, was coming in any case, as wood supplies receded farther and farther from the tracks. The cutting of Sussex oaks for England's wooden walls yielded nothing to the timber felling that went on for years in America to provide daily fuel for 10,000 locomotives and more; and into the half-inch iron fireboxes went many thousand cords of superb wood as well as green wood, hemlock and hornbeam. A good wood could evaporate up to 2½ times its own weight of water.

A cord was 128 cubic feet; that might be anything from 2,000 to 4,000lb in weight according to the wood, but it was the unit of purchase. On only a rough estimate, American-type 4-4-0s in the USA consumed at least 75 million cords in 40 years. Wood-burning was no sinecure for the fireman, for quite ordinary runs with 150-ton passenger trains at 40mph average could mean 160lb of wood fired per mile; and that took some doing.

Apart from roads like the Philadelphia & Reading that had always used anthracite (good stuff, not the culm dust with Wootton firebox of later years), the use of bituminous coals with decreasing wood stocks at economic prices was given a fillip by the steel firebox, which came into trial use in 1861. Boxes built 1861-63 were shown by 1869 to have an unexpired life of seven to eight years, and after a favourable Master Mechanics report of that year a rapid increase was made over the four or five hundred boxes by that time in service.

With the substitution of coal for wood, there disappeared that great symbol of the American-type — the enormous balloon stack containing one or other of the 60-odd forms of spark arrester actually tried, a small

Left: A Pacific No 1246 on Green Mountain Railway, one of the many North American steam preservation facilities. P B Whitehouse

Below: Denver & Rio Grande RR 3ft-gauge 2-8-2 No 473 preserved (with false balloon stack) for seasonal fan-train working between Durango and Silverton (Colo). It is the last remaining US narrow-gauge railway in regular company operation and a popular facility with passengers, whose total now tops 100,000 a year. P B Whitehouse

percentage of the 1,000 different patents. This fitting was seen to be essential long before the time of the 4-4-0, in fact from 1832 when $60,000 in paper money being carried in an open car on the Newcastle & Frenchtown was fired by sparks from the locomotive. Around 1860, extended smokeboxes began to appear, and eased the spark throwing to some extent.

Keeping at full heat a fire consuming two tons or more of wood in an hour needed a blast pipe nozzle no more than 3½in in diameter, though almost universally from 1855 to 1870 two nozzles of around 2½in diameter were used with 16in cylinders, and two of 1⅞in with 15in cylinders. Well might a celebrated locomotive engineer write in the 1860s that each exhaust blast went off like a rifle. Distinct from English practice, the nozzles were very low down in the smokebox, and petticoats extended downwards from the stack.

Well on into the coal-burning era the boiler plates were extremely thin for the pressure used, and the factor of safety was below the levels acceptable in Europe. As a result, along with the often rough working and infrequent inspection (this was before the days of the Interstate Commerce Commission's Bureau of Inspection), boiler explosions were comparatively numerous. This was a feature of the American railroad scene until the end of steam; even as late as the years of the 1939-45 war there were between four and eight locomotive boiler explosions a year, compared with 15 to 25 a year in the 1860s. Boiler pressures of 120lb in the 1860s got plates of only ¼in iron for 4ft diameter, or $\frac{5}{16}$in when the rear end of the barrel was tapered up wagon-top fashion.

Most boilers had front-end throttles until around 1870, despite the presence of a large dome, usually on the firebox top. Mechanically driven pump feed was obligatory, there being no alternative until 1861, when Sellers got a manufacturing licence from Sharp Stewart in England for the Giffard type of injector, and sold over 2,000 in the first year.

Another great feature of American practice that came with the Rogers 4-4-0 was the bar frame. There had been crude bar frames before, and there were plate frames before and after; but by 1855-56 the bar frame as understood in later years had become almost universal. Throughout the time of the American-type engine, it gave no trouble, for spliced joints did not loosen much when piston thrusts were only around 26,000lb and axle loads were about 10 tons. Only with the increases to over 50,000lb and 20 tons in the 1890s did the bolted sections of the bar frame require incessant maintenance attention.

Simplicity in the American 4-4-0 came mainly from the iron bar frames, to which were attached two outside cylinders of 15in to 17in diameter, with flat slide valves on top, and three-point suspension gained by equalising the coupled springs down each side and leaving the leading truck springs on their own. The spring arrangement gave easy movement, and maximum possibility for the wheels to follow the numerous irregularities in the lightly laid track, very often without ballast of any kind. A not unknown occurrence was for a pair of wheels to be derailed and then become rerailed before the driver had awoken to the fact and applied the brake and shut the throttle. Fortunately, as the Rogers-type 4-4-0 was coming in and sizes were going up, the old American strap rails were going out, or had already gone on many

roads; but the after effects of them and the light track construction lasted many years. Three-point suspension had been patented by Harrison in 1838, with a revision in 1842; but the patents had expired by the time the American-type really got going.

The whole riding was further improved by the long distance between the leading drivers and the front truck, which permitted a connecting-rod length seven or eight times the crank throw, and so minimised the upward thrusts on the slidebars and the side-to-side disturbing forces; the long wheelbase itself contributed to easier riding.

By 1860 another practice was in vogue that lasted until the twilight of steam 70 years later. That was the casting of one cylinder and valve chest with half the saddle supporting the smokebox. A saddle support itself had first been seen in 1848 on a McQueen 4-4-0 of pre-Rogers form, but the incorporation of the cylinder with half the saddle was a Baldwin innovation of 1857.

Canadian Pacific Railways No 2317 of a standard 4-6-2 type introduced in the early 1920s and built over a long period.
P B Whitehouse

It lasted more or less until the coming of the cast-steel integral locomotive bed in the late 1920s. There was full access to the slide valves simply by removing a dozen bolts and lifting off the cast-iron cover.

The inside Stephenson gear, always with marine-type links, had transverse rocking shafts to transmit the motion outside; again, everything was accessible because of the bar frames. Rogers adopted this gear in 1849, before his first American-type; other builders adopted it only gradually over the next five or six years, and some used the Gooch stationary-link motion as an intermediate stage. After 1855 non-Stephenson gear engines were rare. The long distance from front drivers to truck also permitted long eccentric rods, sometimes up to 6ft, which produced very even valve events.

Not so blatantly visible as the balloon stack and enormous oil-burning headlamps, the coupled wheels were just as characteristic a detail of the American 4-4-0. Well under one per cent were forged; the remaining 99 per cent until the 1880s were of cast iron, even with tread diameters as great as 78 inches; and from the 1851-52 beginnings until after the civil war the great majority of coupled-wheel tyres also were of cast iron, with chilled tread. Only with the coming of steel tyres did the cast types disappear; and it was time they did, for in the endeavour to make the cast-iron type stronger the thickness had got up to 3½in and the weight was enormous for the general size of the engines. A 6ft wheel-and-axle pair with cast-iron centres and cast-iron tyres weighed around 7,000lb in an engine of no more than 20,000lb axle load.

The normal severe and long-lasting winter temperatures, which not only affected ferrous materials but also froze the roadbed solid, led to regular annual epidemics of wheel centre and tyre breakages; and a common winter sight was an engine at work with several cracked spokes — not hair cracks, either, but real full splits asunder.

45

Left: Virginia & Truckee RR No 11, an 1872
Baldwin, which saw service with the M-G-M
film unit and was afterwards shown by the
Railway and Locomotive Historical Society in
America at the 1969 centenary celebration of
the first transcontinental link-up at Promontory.
B Reed

Below: Traditional 4-4-0 'William Mason' of
Baltimore & Ohio Railroad, pictured at
Baltimore in 1952. J M Jarvis

An early development was the one-piece cast-iron truck wheel without separate tyre. The same wheels were used for freight wagons and some passenger cars, so the production was large enough to justify investment of considerable capital in research and plant; prior to 1870 a 33in disc wheel could be made for 20 dollars, including the slow cooling, and its ½in chill on the tread would normally last for well over 50,000 miles. But the unmachined treads were not always perfectly circular, so that the generally smooth movement on good track could still be disturbed by chatter.

However, light tracks, light construction, and general operating requirements prevented any high speeds. It is doubtful whether any true American-type ever topped 65mph before the 1880s, and even a mile a minute was rare. There were few tracks that could take that speed; in the 1860s a schedule of 42mph was something to be written about, for it might involve a peak not far short of 60mph.

The amount of polished brass, including a 30 to 60lb bell, and polished copper was extensive, and was supplemented by the shining purple of the Russian iron lagging sheets; few, if any, of the American-type 4-4-0s had the polished or painted wood lagging strips of English locomotives, though they had been seen in the States in the 1830s and early 1840s. Additional were numerous ornamental scrolls and devices and two to four brass flagstaffs, and a lavish display of colour painting that put Stroudley's efforts on the Brighton line in England into the Black Five class.

New construction of the real American-type went down sharply in the early 1880s. Although in essence the principles of wheelbase spacing, machinery arrangement and suspension remained, the introduction of steel frames, cast-steel wheel centres, great increase in boiler size and heating surface, and, above all, the suppression of brass, copper and colour, led to a complete change to brute force instead of elegance in appearance.

Deterioration in appearance came first around 1878 when the Philadelphia & Reading introduced camelback 4-4-0s with Wootton grates four times the normal area; but mechanically the Pennsy was again the leader in change, with its K-class of 1882, in which the enlarged boiler was placed 12in to 15in higher than had been known before, and the grate was spread out over the top

bars of the frame instead of being dropped between. A few of the true American-type, constructed in the 1870s and early 1880s, continued to run until at least 1948, and a few are preserved but none restored to the glories of the 1850s and 1860s. One fine example of 1857 construction did remain until 1942, and was then sacrificed in a war-time scrap drive.

Above:
A distinctive feature of engines on early American railways, which were largely unfenced, and particularly of the 4-4-0s was the cowcatcher (or pilot) shown in this engraving from the 'Graphic' of October 11, 1873.
Illustrated London News

Left: A model in the London Science Museum of a traditional American-type 4-4-0 built by William R Lendrum, Scranton. Science Museum London

THE AMERICAN MALLETS

From the first 334,000lb 0-6-6-0 in 1903, Mallet articulated locomotives in the USA were 'the biggest locomotive in the world', far surpassing all Garratts, and culminating in the 340-ton (English) Big Boy 4-8-8-4s of the Union Pacific in 1941. That weight was for the engine alone; combined engine and tender total was 535 English tons, or just on 1,200,000lb. Several other classes in the 1930s and 1940s topped the million-pound mark with tender, but apart from the special Erie and Virginian triplex models, only three got above 700,000lb engine weight.

Among notable holders of the 'largest', meaning 'heaviest', title from 1903 were the Baltimore & Ohio 0-6-6-0 No 2400, the Erie 0-8-8-0s of 1907 (the only three Mallets with Wootten fireboxes), the first Southern Pacific oil-burning 2-8-8-2s of 1909, the Santa Fe's rebuilt 2-10-2s with flexible boiler joints in 1911, the Virginian 2-10-10-2s of 1918, and the Northern Pacific's Z5-class 2-8-8-4s of 1929-30 which had the largest grate area ever (182sq ft). These examples exclude the Erie triplex engines of 1913-16 and the one Virginian triplex of 1916, but all four of them were Mallet tank engines, the only standard-gauge examples in the States, though there were narrow-gauge Mallet tanks for some of the Colorado lines.

From the mid-1920s the title holders were no longer four-cylinder compounds but four-cylinder simple expansion; they retained the system of articulation evolved by Anatole Mallet in 1884. His system of compounding dated back to 1874.

Adopted first by the then newly formed Alco combine after close study of the Gotthard-line 0-6-6-0s and other European Mallets of lighter weight, the B & O engine was 17 per cent heavier than the biggest rigid-framed engine of the time, and its adhesion weight was 40 per cent more. For 18 months after its completion the future of the Mallet in North America was dubious; but the continued good behaviour of that 12-wheeler throughout the year following its release from the St Louis Exposition of 1904 led to adoption of the format by other roads for steepgrade pusher service, and then for drag freight work.

The original 0-6-6-0 wheel notation died out for new construction after 80 had been built; the larger 0-8-8-0 went to a total of 150. In a sense that finished the definite banking designs, though in practice engines with leading and trailing trucks often did pusher service. The front trucks gave rather easier riding at 20mph upwards; trailing trucks gave better air-flow and ashpan conditions. And so extension began with 2-6-6-0s, 2-6-6-2s, 2-8-8-0s and 2-8-8-2s, all of which had appeared by 1909.

Few Mallets were ever built specifically for passenger service, perhaps only the Southern Pacific's 2-6-6-2s, soon rebuilt to 4-6-6-2, and a few rebuilds on the Santa Fe; on steep-grade sections normal Mallets often were employed on passenger trains, either as head-end power or as pushers.

A typical American 4-4-0 with
wood-burning chimney, as built in huge
numbers in the 1880-1890 period, passing
through six-gun territory in Florida USA.
Picturepoint

General designs settled down with remarkably little trouble, partly because speed in the first few years rarely got as high as 25mph. Only one or two roads, like the Santa Fe, laid up trouble for themselves with flexibly jointed boilers, semi-flexible fireboxes, and rebuilds of two old rigid-frame engines into one Mallet; though for years Baldwin pushed its sectional boiler with smoke chamber and feedwater heater compartment without benefit to users. Reason for the variations was the sudden surge in locomotive length with the incorporation of end trucks, on which designers had not ruminated.

Mallet construction from 1909-10 was extensive, but a further fillip was given after the USA came tardily into the 1914-18 war, for then the United States Railway Administration standardised further wartime construction on half-a-dozen new locomotive types, including light and heavy 2-8-8-2 Mallets that were quite a success. Later, some railroads, like the Norfolk & Western, based their own Mallets on the USRA designs, and that parentage could be traced even on the last-built N & W 2-8-8-2s of 1948-52.

Until the early 1920s, limits to the application of big Mallets came from the number of freight cars not fitted with the latest pattern of MCB centre coupler, and starting efforts around 100,000lb pulled out too many drawbars with an unassisted Mallet at the head of the train. On the other hand, those were the days of immense coal trains requiring, say, a couple of 2-10-10-2 bankers at the rear and one 2-8-8-2 at the head to get 15,000 tons up 1 in 50 at around 8mph, with a total coal consumption approximating to 15 tons an hour. Such trains commonly were of high-capacity limited-route wagons.

Nevertheless, by 1922 the locomotive itself, rather than centre couplers, was forming the limitation; the compound system applied to the long articulated layout, with the two steam circuits as part of one system, had reached its peak, not only in mechanical matters such as the size of the low-pressure cylinders, which in the Virginian 2-10-10-2s were 48in bore, but in the sluggishness of steam and exhaust flows, which practically prevented top speeds above 25mph; that meant drag hauls scarcely above 14mph, and little over half that on steep grades, even with pushers.

Compound development reached its peak in size with the 10 Virginian 2-10-10-2s Nos 800-09 of 1918, which weighed 684,000lb engine only and had the largest heating surface ever, 8,606sq ft. Even for Mallets they were pot-bellied, with a boiler barrel 9ft 10in diameter; they were the only ten-coupled Mallets built new as such. Compound Mallets built from 1919 to 1924 were more modest and were mainly 2-8-8-2s. Only the N & W thereafter developed the compound to get advantage from higher pressure; to 1924 few Mallets had above 210lb.

By that time higher effective freight train speeds were becoming essential, partly for quick delivery of perishables, but also for a straight increase in line capacity to take the growing traffic of all types. Mallets had given an increase in capacity over Mikados and 2-10-0s of earlier years, but in the early 1920s there were several instances where more-modern simple-expansion 2-10-2s, when fitted with boosters, increased the line capacity compared with Mallets of nearly twice the size, simply because the higher speed uphill more than counterbalanced the heavier load that could be taken by the Mallets.

Next stage was initiated in 1924 with 25 Alco-built four-cylinder simple 2-8-8-2s on the Chesapeake & Ohio. General increase in boiler pressures in the States was another two or three years off, for the 240lb of the USRA designs had not been repeated, and the C & O machines had only 205lb. The increase in practicable speed which they brought was notable, and they could be got up to a maximum of 35mph on suitable sections, which meant that 14-15mph drag freight schedules could be accelerated to 20-22mph; yet the normal output of those engines was not more than 3,300 indicated horsepower at 20mph.

They were not the first simple-expansion Mallets, for the Pennsylvania built a 50 per cent max cut-off 2-8-8-0 in 1919, and that itself followed eight years after another 'one-off' 2-8-8-2 in 1911. Nothing came of those two prototypes, and otherwise the Pennsy had only a handful of compound 2-8-8-2s. The four-cylinder simple-expansion 2-8-8-2 soon spread to the Great Northern, Rio Grande, Southern and other roads, but only to a total of 86, for it was overtaken by developments that followed Lima's application of a four-wheel trailing truck to rigid-frame locomotives, so that by 1928 the Mallet also was appearing with two-axle trucks.

Strangely, almost the first application was a 'reverse -order' 4-8-8-2 — the new breed of cab-in-front SP Mallets for the Sierra section, which began after a 15-year gap since the construction of the last compounds for the route. With that layout, the oil-burning firebox could be carried above the drivers, and so the four-wheel truck was used mainly for better guiding at the leading end. As many as 195 of the 4-8-8-2 cab-in-front engines were acquired between 1928 and 1944, with a gradual increase in weight from 481,000 to 658,000lb.

First of the notable four-wheel trailing truck installations was to the 12 Yellowstone 2-8-8-4s of the Northern Pacific in 1929-30. To burn lignite from the railroad's own mines a grate of 182sq ft was provided; the evaporative heating surface of 7,673sq ft was exceeded only by the old Virginian 2-10-10-2s, which had the A-type superheater, whereas the NP engines had the E-type equipment.

In this second stage of Mallet development, the simple expansion, higher pressures, and greater attention to valves, valve motion, and boiler output increased substantially the effective speed and power compared with the best of the older compounds; moreover, slipping was considerably decreased as the back and front steam systems were separate and had no intersurges. One major failing of the big Mallet still remained; the poor riding and instability. Simple-expansion engines could attain 35 to 40mph and occasionally more, but the riding then was almost dangerous and the imposed track stresses very high. There was a consequential deleterious effect on the bar frames, despite the size to cope with axle loads of 70,000lb and piston thrusts above 130,000lb.

Integral cast frames, dating from around 1928 for large locomotives, eased the frame position, though not the actual stresses coming on them. The principle of the Mallet articulation was that the rear group was the fixed unit, and the whole front group pivoted about it like a heavily laden multi-axle Bissell truck, with the front end of the boiler resting on curved slides, and with the additional complication that the Bissell was driven. Movement of the whole front group was inherently unstable, but the effects could be tolerated up to 30-35mph.

Simple-expansion Mallets had improved one aspect in that both steam and exhaust pipes attached to the rear cylinder group could be carried on the boiler and so needed no universal or flexible sliding joints; the front engine still needed such joints for live steam and exhaust.

In the early 1930s lateral-motion devices giving up to one inch each way of spring-cushioned side movement were adopted for the leading drivers on all new Mallets, and more engines for fast freight also had four-wheel leading trucks with spring-controlled side movement instead of swing links. But only when precision-machined and precision-fitted flat supports for the front end of the boiler, and articulation joints that prevented 'rock 'n roll', were added in the UP 4-6-6-4 Challengers in 1935 did the Mallet become a safe mile-a-minute proposition, and the third and final stage of American Mallet development begin.

For sheer fast passenger and fast freight work the Challengers themselves were never surpassed, though many similar 4-6-4-4s followed on lines such as the Delaware & Hudson, Western Pacific, and DRGW, and about 215 were built altogether. The N & W got equally satisfactory riding, high speeds, and a drawbar output up to 6,300hp, with a 2-6-6-4 layout, built by the road 1936-50. The design was developed also into the huge 4-8-8-4s of the UP and NP, and they also were no mean performers in speed, having been designed for 70mph top.

Transition from first to second stage in Mallet development had brought the type out of the pure pusher stage and put it into the drag-freight long-haul range, and even just into the manifest freight speeds as they were in the early 1920s. In the 1930s those speeds had to go up sharply, and it was the third stage in development which permitted that to be done — and, incidentally, diminished the new construction of large rigid-frame 2-10-4s.

The great adhesion and power of third-stage Mallets could still be used in pusher service over crucial sections where an economic survey showed the great capital investment was warranted. Several were so used to help traffic in the 1939-45 war, including the Big Boys themselves up the 30 miles of average 1 in 85 grade to Sherman summit, working there for a couple of hours or more at full throttle and 65 per cent cut-off, with speed staying between 10 and 15mph.

The C & O, with an allowable axle load of 78,500lb on some routes, adopted the 2-6-6-6 layout to get a grate area of 135sq ft; but the UP and DRGW got larger grates above more heavily laden four-wheel trucks. No other six-coupled Mallet approached the C & O adhesion weight of 471,000lb except the handful built to the same design for the Virginian. The C & O machines were checked at above 7,000 drawbar horsepower.

Strangely, the last Mallets to be built in the USA for home service were compounds. The N & W had never given up compound propulsion or the 2-8-8-2 wheel arrangement for its drag coal trains; and, being the last Class 1 railroad to continue at full blast with steam traction, built at its Roanoke shops through 1948-52 a series of 30 locomotives which, though they had practically the same cylinder size and wheel diameter as the engines built in 1918-19, had 300lb boiler pressure, 16 per cent greater weight, and advanced valve motion. The 39in low-pressure cylinders were notable in having 18in piston valves, probably the largest diameter ever put into a steam locomotive.

The last batch of engines brought the N & W total of 2-8-8-2s to 220. The company's charged price of $260,000 per engine and tender (incidentally 2.65 times the cost of the first 2-8-8-2s in 1919) was cheap at a time when Lima was getting from the Louisville & Nashville $255,000 for a 2-8-4 roller-bearing engine and tender.

As the largest steam locomotives ever, the Big Boys deserve a word. They were built in two batches, in 1941 and 1944. The latter weighed 772,000lb and had a 14-wheel tender scaling 437,000lb all on, giving a total of 1,209,000lb. With a total wheelbase of 117ft 7in and an overall length of 127ft, they were given 135ft turntables at the principal points. The pressure of 300lb was the highest ever used in a simple-expansion Mallet, but as the cylinders were only 23¾ in bore the piston

One of the 2-6-6-6 Mallets of very high adhesion weight and over 7,000 drawbar hp built by the Chesapeake & Ohio, in this instance, for the Virginian Railroad. C&O/B&O Railroads

thrust did not rise above 133,000lb, a long way off the maximum of 219,000lb in a rigid-frame locomotive. Next heaviest engine was the C & O 2-6-6-6 at 724,500lb, and then came the NP Class Z5 2-8-8-4 at 723,500lb. Big Boys and Challengers also had the biggest tenders among Mallets, with 21,000 imperial gallons of water and 25 long tons of coal.

In the 49 years from 1903 about 3,100 standard-gauge Mallets in 21 different wheel arrangements were built in the States for home service, plus the two types of triplex engines, and a few Mallet tank and tender engines of 3ft gauge for the Uintah Railway and some logging roads. Just over 40 per cent of all engines were 2-6-6-2s. Of the standard-gauge engines nearly 2,400 were compounds, so that while the later simple-expansion engines made a tremendous difference to fast freight working on a few major railroads, they by no means changed the general picture of main-line freight working throughout the USA.

Right: Milwaukee Road 2-6-6-2 on the Olympic Hiawatha train at Tacoma, Wash, in July 1952.
All J M Jarvis

**Below:
Southern Pacific's 'reverse-order' 4-8-8-2 Mallet of 1928, of which nearly 200 were built permitted the mounting of the oil burning firebox over one set of drivers.**
Southern Pacific Transportation Company.

GREAT AMERICAN PASSENGER TRAINS

At the dawn of the twentieth century the 4-4-2, or Atlantic, dominated the US motive power scene, having then recently superseded the 4-4-0 in order to obtain increased boiler capacity to cope with increasingly heavy passenger stock. First truly introduced on the Atlantic Coast Line in 1894, the 4-4-2 was soon adopted by many railroads, including some in the west, but it became particularly associated with railroads serving the Eastern seaboard, namely, the Pennsylvania Railroad, the Philadelphia & Reading Central Railroad of New Jersey, and the ACL itself.

Many of the early American 4-4-2s were not objects of beauty, some being of the camelback or Mother Hubbard type, in which the fireman was banished to a vestigial cab at the rear to stoke the huge Wootten firebox. As boilers got ever bigger, after about 1905 the driver was reunited with his fireman and the curious camelback form mercifully disappeared. Nevertheless, 4-6-0s of that pattern operated in commuter service until 1954 on the Central Railroad of New Jersey, which obtained from the Brooks Locomotive Works in 1902 three camelback Atlantics with 7ft drivers and 82sq ft of grate.

Quite a large proportion of American 4-4-2s were compounds. Many of the earlier examples built in the 1890s and early 1900s operated on the Vauclain principle with high- and low-pressure (outside) cylinders one above the other and cast together in one piece, and having a common crosshead. Few if any tandem compounds were built for passenger service (as they were for freight) and during about 1904-6 quite a number of Cole so-called balanced compounds were built, both with divided and unified cylinder drive. The same principle was applied to some early 4-6-2s, for example, on the Northern Pacific, but the advent of super-heating virtually ousted compounding overnight as far as concerned new passenger locomotive construction.

Nevertheless, the Atcheson Topeka & Santa Fe combined compounding and superheaters in 4-4-2s and 4-6-2s built as late as 1910 and 1911 respectively. Initiated in the USA by the same redoubtable Cole, in 1905, the superheater was becoming well-established by about 1910 and from, say, 1912, superheated two-cylinder simple-expansion locomotives became the almost invariable standard for new American passenger locomotive construction until the end of the steam era.

The most outstanding American 4-4-2s were those of the Pennsylvania RR, which, almost solely in the USA, designed, developed and built its own locomotives; they were further distinguished by the Belpaire firebox. The first PRR 4-4-2 (Class E1) was built in 1899 and there followed from its Altoona, Pa, shops several varieties, including Cole compounds, and a de Glehn compound 4-4-2 was experimentally purchased from France.

Although a 4-6-2 was purchased for experiment in 1907, PRR 4-4-2 development continued and in 1910 three large-boilered engines using saturated steam (Class E6) were built. They eclipsed in haulage capacity the first PRR-designed 4.6.2s built the following year which weighed 22 per cent more. Superheating was in vogue at that time (c 1910) and it was soon to revolutionise locomotive practice the world over. As a result, a superheater 4-4-2 (Class E6s) was built in 1914 which put out a phenomenal maximum of 2,448 indicated horsepower, making it effectively the most powerful four-coupled locomotive ever built. Eighty of the PRR E6 class were built and extensively used east of Harrisburg between New York and Philadelphia. All survived the 1939-45 war, and three lasted until as recently as 1955.

No doubt inspired by the PRR's four-coupled power-pack were four 4-4-4s built by the Philadelphia & Reading in 1914-15. The first American exponent of the trailing four-wheeled truck, the new P & R engines had Wootten fireboxes with grates of a monstrous 108sq ft, scarcely to be excelled even by a 4-8-4. Very unstable in operation, the rare machines were soon rebuilt as 4-4-2s and never matched their Pennsy counterparts.

With the appearance of the Reading 4-4-4s and the last PRR E6s in 1915, four-coupled locomotive develop-

Southern Pacific streamlined 4-8-4
No 447 at Los Angeles Union station
in 1947. V Goldberg collection

Florida East Coast Railway 4-8-2 No 442
at Miami in 1940. W Monypeny (C L
Andrews)

ment in the USA almost ceased — but not quite. Just 20 years later, after the resurgence from the economic depression of the early 1930s, a pair of gaudy orange-and-red streamlined new 4-4-2s with 300lb boiler pressure appeared on the Chicago Milwaukee & St Paul RR in 1935. They had been evolved to counter the rival Burlington Route's new high-speed diesel train and whisk a lightweight luxury five-car train 400 miles in 400 minutes, with scheduled maxima of 100mph en route.

Unlike all previous US non-compound 4-4-2s, cylinder drive was on the leading coupled axle and the wheelbase was well spaced out. Oil firing imposed no limit on sustained maximum output as it did on the hand-fired Pennsy 4-4-2. An experimental 4-4-4 also appeared on the Baltimore & Ohio at the same time and there were several smaller examples of this type on the Canadian Pacific north of the 49th parallel, but the outbreak of war a few years later rendered all those light four-coupled machines white elephants for the rest of their short lives.

The Pennsy E6s set a commendable standard in that its superb boiler could supply any amount of steam the cylinders demanded; but it still had one severe limitation — adhesion. First introduced in the USA as early as 1850, the 4-6-0 type was already rapidly becoming obsolescent except in secondary service by the end of the nineteenth century. In a 4-6-0 it was not readily possible to combine a large wide firebox with large-diameter driving wheels.

During the early 1900s, a number of 2-6-2 tender engines, or Prairies, were built for express passenger service. Probably the most outstanding of them were ten with 79in drivers built by the Brooks works (by then a part of the American Locomotive Company) in 1905 for the Lake Shore & Michigan Southern in 1905. They held

the then highly ephemeral distinction of being the largest passenger engines in the world until superseded by even larger 4-6-2s on the same railroad in 1907. A subsequent batch (1906) ranked among the earliest applications of Walschaerts valve gear in passenger service in North America. Having an adhesive factor as high as almost 6.0, they should have been very sure-footed machines, but instability at speed because of the leading pony truck led to the rapid fall from favour of the 2-6-2 type in high-speed service, although smaller-wheeled Prairies lasted on the Northern Pacific until the end of steam around 1958. A leading bogie was obviously necessary.

The 4-6-2, or Pacific, made its effective debut on the Missouri Pacific in 1902 and on the Chesapeake & Ohio a few weeks later; it had become very widespread and had increased dramatically in size and capacity by 1910. Large-boilered saturated-steam 4-6-2s with piston valves and Walschaerts valve gear built by American Loco in 1907 for the NYC and PRR systems (for trial) could be said to be the progenitor of the modern American steam passenger locomotive. The earliest 4-6-2s had inside Stephenson valve gear and inboard steamchests, or even slide valves, but external Walschaerts or Baker valve gear and piston valves soon became standard.

Most outstanding of the almost innumerable US 4-6-2 designs was the Pennsylvania K4s first introduced in 1914, of which no fewer than 425 ultimately appeared. It was essentially a six-coupled enlargement of the E6s 4-4-2 and although several latterly were updated with roller bearings, poppet valves and so on, it was basically the rugged piston-valve 4-6-2 of 1914 (with the later addition of a mechanical stoker) that was still handling the backbone of the PRR passenger services 30 years later.

The K4s ran with a variety of tenders of increasing size. Whereas the original engine had a small one with capacity of 7,000 US gallons of water and 12½ short tons of coal, some later engines hauled immense 16-wheelers holding 24,400 gallons and 25 tons of fuel. It was symptomatic of the increasingly heavy trains hauled and the longer distances run between engine changes. An attempt to develop the K4s yet one stage further into the K5, with higher boiler pressure but retaining the same 70sq ft of hand-fired grate, met with little success and only two such engines, one with Caprotti poppet valve gear, were built.

By the time the last new 4-6-2 entered service on the Pennsylvania RR in 1929, a development manifested on the rival New York Central, which had itself progressively developed the 4-6-2 for over 20 years in many respects rendered obsolete the Pacific in heavy-duty passenger service. In 1927 the NYC placed in service the first of 275 4-6-4 Hudsons on its highly competitive (with the PRR) New York-Chicago run. The trailing four-wheeled truck permitted a larger (mechanically fired) grate and much greater power than in the hand-fired Pennsy 4-6-2.

The NYC 4-6-4s themselves were improved considerably over their eleven-year constructional period. The final examples could develop 25 per cent greater maximum power for a mere five per cent more weight. The improvement was achieved mainly through incorporating a combustion chamber in the firebox and the extensive use of high-tensile nickel alloy steel in the boiler plates and running gear. The earlier engines had Walschaerts valve gear which was later replaced by Baker gear — a peculiarly American derivative more suitable to cope with maximum valve travel lengths of the order of 8½ inches. Later engines also had disc or Boxpok driving wheel centres designed to reduce weight and inflict less punishment on the track. As with the Pennsy 4-6-2s, tender size steadily increased.

Although the best known, the NYC Hudsons were by no means the largest US 4-6-4s. In the late 1930s, streamlined high-speed examples with 84in drivers were built for the CM & St P and Chicago and North Western Railroads. When new, the engines regularly exceeded 100mph, and almost mythical tales were told of them. The heaviest and last were five built by the Baldwin Locomotive Works in 1948 for the Chesapeake & Ohio; they had sophisticated Franklin poppet-valve gear and weighed 198 tons apiece without tender.

Many American locomotives of the early 20th century were of decidedly austere appearance, but that was certainly not true of later machines. The visit of the British GWR 4-6-0 *King George V* to the USA in 1927 impressed many US railroad officials and there was thereafter a conscious effort in many quarters to conceal extraneous pipework beneath boiler jackets and to improve appearance generally. Nevertheless, American engines retained a handsome, if essentially functional, appearance to the end. The huge boilers of later years left little room inside loading gauges for them to be so obviously cluttered with such protruberances as feed-water heaters and air pumps, as had been prominent in the early 1920s.

In time, the limitations of six-coupled wheels, even when backed up by adequate boiler capacity, began to make themselves felt. The 4-8-2 featured relatively little

in front-rank passenger service, being more of a mixed-traffic/fast-freight type, of which the somewhat conservative NYC and PRR concerns operated huge fleets having drivers of 69in to 72in which were frequently pressed into passenger service. The Great Northern had some 4-8-2s with cylindrical Vanderbilt tenders (they had some almost identical counterparts on the Canadian National) built by Baldwin in 1923; they handled the crack GNR Oriental Limited for some years.

By the time passenger loadings generally demanded eight-coupled wheels the so-called Super Power concept, with four-wheeled trailing truck, had arrived. The result was the 4-8-4, which epitomised the final heroic period of North America steam railroading, from 1930 to 1950. A passenger 4-8-4 of, say, 1940 represented a tremendous advance over its 4-6-2 counterpart of only 20 years earlier. It would develop about 60,000lb of tractive effort compared to 40,000lb, although its cylinder dimensions could still be much the same because of a rise in boiler pressure from 200lb to 300lb per square inch. In place of the bar frames and separately cast cylinders of the 4-6-2, all those parts would be cast together as a single unit in the 4-8-4, which would also very likely have the refinement of roller bearings in place of plain journals.

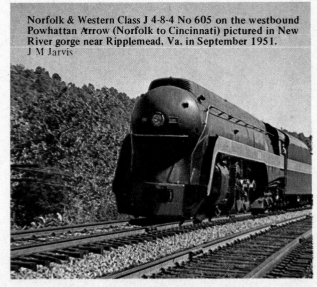

Norfolk & Western Class J 4-8-4 No 605 on the westbound Powhattan Arrow (Norfolk to Cincinnati) pictured in New River gorge near Ripplemead, Va, in September 1951.
J M Jarvis

The three big American locomotive builders Alco, Baldwin and Lima all built appreciable numbers of 4-8-4s, as did several railroads in their own shops. They were all remarkably uniform as to the bare essentials, having two cylinders (except for one obscure experimental unit on the NYC) and round-topped fireboxes, except for one series with Belpaire on the Great Northern. One of the few major variations was in valve gear — Walschaerts versus Baker, although one 4-8-4 for the NYC in 1946 was given poppet valves. The final series of 4-8-4s on the Union Pacific were unusually equipped with double blastpipes and double chimneys.

A few 4-8-4s were streamlined in vogue with their period of construction, almost entirely for publicity purposes rather than to save horsepower at high speed. Among the most striking of the streamliners were the great orange-and-red oil burners of the Southern Pacific, which hauled the SP's Daylights down the California coast well into the 1950s. The black bullet-nosed 4-8-4s of the Norfolk & Western with 70in drivers developed a record 80,000lb tractive effort without booster and could exceed 100mph with ease.

The heavier US 4-8-4s represented probably the largest high-speed steam motive power on rails possible within the generous confines of the US loading gauge. No greater diameter of boiler could be got in, which fixed an upper limit on maximum steaming capacity. The largest 4-8-4s could develop 6,000-7,000 cylinder horsepower, of which 4,000-5,000hp emerged at the drawbar. The massive and robust machines were exploited ruthlessly both in power output and endurance. The oil-burning 4-8-4s of the Atcheson Topeka & Santa Fe, the *heaviest* ever at 231 long tons without tender in the final Baldwin series of 1943-4, regularly ran right through the 1,791 miles between Kansas City and Los Angeles with six refuelling and 16 water stops, and 11 crew changes.

Facilities were developed to achieve long through runs with coal-burning steam power also. Refuelling was carried out by overhead chutes at stops, where the ashpan was emptied and the fire cleaned. The latter-day 4-8-4s of the New York Central, delivered in 1945-6, when new regularly ran the 928 miles throughout between Harmon (33 miles north of New York) and Chicago. With the provision of water pick-up apparatus, rare in the USA, the engines carried no less than 41 long tons of coal, thus necessitating only one coaling stop on the run. Equipped with every modern device, the NYC 4-8-4s were the most intensively utilised steam locomotives ever built. When new, representatives were pitted against diesel-electrics to determine future NYC motive power policy and covered over a quarter of a million miles apiece per annum, a truly amazing figure!

One curious departure from the norm at that late stage was the short-lived Pennsylvania Duplex 4-4-4-4. Later 4-8-4s had attained such a size that they were beginning to suffer self-strangulation from their huge cylinders and limited valves, while the corresponding heavy machinery revolving and reciprocating at high speeds was mutually destructive of both the locomotive and the track upon which it ran. The 52 PRR 4-4-4-4s were thus 4-8-4s with four small cylinders and lighter moving parts and two sets of four-coupled wheels. Excessive slipping and high maintenance costs associated with the complicated poppet valve gear only facilitated the rapid influx of diesels while the engines were still new.

A modern American steam passenger locomotive of the 1940s weighed about twice as much as its counterpart of the early 1900s, but such were the technological advances made in the intervening period, particularly superheating but also in metallurgy, that it could develop between three and four times more power. For instance, an early non-superheated NYC 120-ton 4-6-2 of 1907 developed a maximum of 16.7 indicated horsepower per long ton (2,000ihp), which was precisely half that of the 210-ton Niagara 4-8-4 of 1945 when worked all out at 7,000ihp.

American locomotives were almost invariably worked at high power outputs, with attendant colossal firing and combustion rates. Under such conditions, boiler thermal efficiencies often sank to 50 per cent and below. Spectacular to witness and to hear in full eruption, such prodigal consumption of increasingly costly coal was a contributory factor to the rapid supersession of steam by diesel-electric in the USA in the late 1940s and early 1950s, when many still new steam machines were consigned to the scrapheap.

Below: Steamlined Hudson-type locomotive introduced in the late 1930s by New York Central for its crack passenger services.
Ian Allan library

THE TWENTIETH CENTURY LIMITED

For many years it was claimed that no stay in the United States was complete unless the tourist had had the opportunity of 'Riding the Century'. Today, alas, the experience is no longer possible, for with the drastic curtailment of American passenger services that has resulted from air and road competition most long-distance trains have ceased any longer to be a paying proposition and many have been withdrawn.

The service originated in June 1902 when the then New York Central & Hudson River Railroad and the Lake Shore & Michigan Southern Railroad introduced an express service over their joint 961-mile route between New York and Chicago; the 20-hour schedule cut four hours from the previous best over the course. The new train was named Twentieth Century Limited. As the names of the two railways indicated, for the first 142 miles, to Albany, the NYC & HRR main line, running due north, ran along the left bank of the Hudson River. At Albany the line turned due west through Syracuse to a course just south of Lakes Ontario and Erie, through Buffalo, where the LS&MSRR took over, to Cleveland and Toledo, after which a cut across country brought the line into Chicago, at the southern end of Lake Michigan.

The proximity of the railway to the water over most of its length prompted the New York Central slogan, 'Water Level Route – You Can Sleep', which the NYC splashed over its timetables and other publicity. The slogan was also a sly dig at the competing Pennsylvania Company, whose Pennsylvania Special (in 1912 renamed the Broadway Limited), was introduced on the same day as the Twentieth Century Limited and on the same 20-hour schedule. The Pennsy train took a shorter 908-mile course through the Allegheny mountains, at the cost of climbing to a summit level of 2,193ft at Gallitzin, west of Altoona, up gradients as steep as 1 in 50, with correspondingly hard effort and noisy exhaust by the locomotives.

Development of the Twentieth Century route was undertaken by the New York Central System, an amalgamation of the New York Central and the Lake Shore lines. In later years the route had the distinction of being the longest four-track main line in the world; there was 474 miles of it continuously from Castleton, just outside New York, to Collinwood, in the suburbs of Cleveland. More recently, however, much of the quadruple trackage has been reduced to ordinary double track, but with frequent crossover roads and suitable signalling to permit eitherway working on both lines.

By contrast, in former days when the Twentieth Century Limited and other expresses reached Syracuse, their route to the passenger station lay, like a tramway, through busy city streets at 15mph, until at long last a new main line to a new station made it possible to abandon this troublesome practice. Steam haulage throughout of the Twentieth Century for the first five years of its life gave way in 1907 to electric operation between the Grand Central Terminal in New York and Wakefield, extended in 1913 to Harmon, nearly 33 miles out.

The cut of four hours below the previous fastest time between New York and Chicago, initiated with the Twentieth Century Limited, introduced a novel system of fare charging. With the previous 28 hours fixed as the standard time, an extra fare of one dollar (later increased to $1.20) was charged for every hour that the passenger saved with the accelerated service. With every subsequent acceleration the supplement was increased, but with the proviso that for every hour that the Twentieth Century might be late in arriving, the passenger was entitled to a corresponding refund. In later years, however, this flexible fare system was replaced by a flat-rate service charge, in addition to the first-class fare and Pullman supplement.

Mention of Pullman brings its reminder that the Twentieth Century Limited was an all-Pullman train. In its early days the coaches were of the Pullman convertible type, in the daytime providing ordinary seating on each side of a central corridor, and at night converted to sleeping cars by pulling the seats together to form lower berths and folding down panels in sides under the ceiling to provide upper berths. At both levels beds were thus arranged lengthwise along the coach sides and curtains were drawn along both sides of the central gangway. In their berths behind the curtains passengers had the uncomfortable task of undressing and getting into bed, and in the morning of getting up and dressing. Washing and shaving had to be performed in communal wash rooms at both ends of each car.

By degrees, however, new Pullman cars were introduced with single and double rooms of various sizes (some oddly described as 'drawing rooms'), and the supplementary Pullman charges were varied according to the size and relative luxury of the accommodation provided. By 1908 wooden coach-bodies were being replaced by all-steel stock, the rear-end observation platforms on the last coach were being replaced by glassed-in observation lounges, and all kinds of other amenities were being introduced.

In the middle 1950s the Twentieth Century Limited had reached the height of its fame. It had become one of a number of 'all-room' trains. The least expensive accommodation was in roomettes, which were tiny single

rooms, dovetailed into one another to make the maximum possible able seats for daytime travel and a quickaction fold-down ready-made-up bed, with its own toilet facilities. Then there were single bedrooms, similarly with beds folding into the walls, but with rather more space; still larger double bedrooms for couples; and 'master rooms', which were suites with their own shower-baths.

The complete normal formation of the Twentieth Century in its heyday included four drawing rooms, four 'compartments', 79 double bedrooms and 30 roomettes, providing sleeping accommodation for just over 200 passengers in nine coaches. In addition there were two restaurant cars, a club lounge and a rear-end observation lounge, a baggage car with sleeping accommodation for off-duty train staff, and a post office and 'express' (Parcels) car. Refreshments could be obtained in a couple of the train lounges as well as in the dining cars.

The size of the staff required to man such a hotel-on-wheels can well be imagined. Including the dining and refreshment car attendants, kitchen crew, a 'porter' for each sleeping car, baggage men, conductor, barber, lady hostess, even a train secretary, and, of course, the enginemen, it could easily run to a total of 30 or more; the need for a special service charge is thereby explained.

For some years the sleeping cars included two which were transferred in Chicago from the New York Central to the Santa Fe Railroad, and worked by Santa Fe Super-Chief train through to Los Angeles, and thus across the United States from the Atlantic to the Pacific coast. But in time air competition put the Los Angeles sleepers out of business, and also reduced the New York-Chicago *clientele* until at last, by the middle 1960s, the proud all-Pullman Twentieth Century had been invaded by 'sleeper coaches'. (In the USA the 'coach' has always been the equivalent of European second class.) Also added were reclining-chair cars — that is, open saloons fitted with tilting seats to ease night-time travel — available, like single and double rooms of the sleeper coaches, at second-class fares, with supplementary and the flat service charges added. This democratisation was unable to generate an economic revival and turned out to be only the prelude to the final

withdrawal of the Twentieth Century Limited in 1970.

In the earliest days of the Twentieth Century Limited its coaches were all of wooden construction, but in course of time the serious casualties caused by the destruction of coaching stock in American accidents led, first, to the introduction of massive steel underframes, and later to all-steel body construction. Also the length of American vehicles, which grew to 85ft or so, resulted in the almost universal adoption of six-wheel bogies to carry them. With such heavy constituents it was common for American Pullman sleeping and dining cars to grow to weights of 70 or 80 tons apiece, with the result that a long-distance express like the Twentieth Century could easily total upwards of 1,000 tons.

In its earlier years, for that reason, it was not unusual for the train to be operated in three or more sections; indeed, it has been known for as many as eight sections of the one train to follow one another along the 961-mile route. But later on additional named trains with but little longer journey times relieved the pressure on the Century, as also did the splitting off of the Boston portion, attached and detached at Albany, into a separate train called the New England States. By degrees the stops at Albany and Syracuse, going west, became halts to pick up passengers only, and at Buffalo no passenger business was done; the previous stop and reversal at Cleveland Union Terminal was cut out by the use of an avoiding line, reducing the overall journey to 958 miles; and the Toledo and Elkhart stops were restricted to setting down only, with corresponding arrangements in the reverse direction.

From its introductory schedule in 1902 of 20 hours in each direction, the Twentieth Century Limited was accelerated in 1908 for a brief period to 18 hours. It was only a brief improvement however and after a serious accident to the rival Pennsylvania Special, whose time also had been cut to 18 hours, there was a reversion to the 20-hour schedule. So matters continued until April 1932, when an 18-hour booking was again essayed, a year later to be cut to 17¾ hours. In June 1938 a further reduction to 16 hours for the first time brought the overall speed to the Twentieth Century up to 60mph, all stops included. In the early part of the 1939-45 war there was a temporary increase to 17 hours, but the 16-hour schedule was restored in the spring of 1946, by which time diesel power had come in to replace the steam locomotives.

Even the 20-hour schedule involved some very fast intermediate times. In the final years the Century was booked in both directions over the 133 miles between Toledo and Elkhart in 111 min at 71.9mph start to stop; from Buffalo to Collinwood (a stop outside Cleveland to change engine crews) the time allowed for the 174.7 miles was 147 minutes and in the reverse direction 148 minutes, at start-to-stop averages of 71.3 and 70.9mph respectively. Buffalo-Collinwood was the longest non-stop part of the journey. A later acceleration brought the Toledo-Elkhart time, with diesel traction, down to 108 minutes, boosting the average speed to 74.1mph.

Such times demanded speeds of well over 80mph for much of the distance, with a train which, even after the introduction of streamlined lightweight coaches, weighed well over 1,000 tons.

As to Twentieth Century Limited motive power, with the relatively light loads of the early years 4-4-0 locomotives (such as the famous No 999) were able to cope. As weight grew there was a progressive change to the 4-4-2 and 4-6-2 wheel arrangements and then to the highly capable Class J3 4-6-4, or Hudson class. With two 22½in by 29in cylinders, 6ft 7in coupled wheels and 275lb/sq in working pressure, the Hudsons could exert a tractive effort of 43,440lb, to which a booster could add 12,100lb for starting. Ample steam was provided by a boiler with 4,187sq ft of heating surfaces and 1,745 sq ft of superheating surface, and a firegrate with an area of 82 sq ft (perhaps needless to say, mechanically fired).

A Hudson in working order weighed 160¾ tons; with a 12-wheel tender carrying nearly 27 tons of coal and 14,000 gallons of water the weight was 300 tons. With the Hudsons the practice began of using the same locomotive unchanged between Harmon, where the changeover from electric haulage took place, and Chicago, a total distance of 925 miles. The water supply was replenished from time to time from track-troughs, and at two points en route the coal supply was topped up from gantries spanning the line. There also, during a brief stop, the engines were given a quick service examination by attendant fitters.

But something bigger and even more imposing came with the advent of the Niagara-class 4-8-4s. These monsters, with 25½in by 32in cylinders but unchanged 6ft 7in coupled wheels and 275lb pressure, had a tractive effort of 61,570lb which needed no boosters; steam was produced in a boiler having 4,827sq ft heating surface, 2,060sq ft superheating surface and a firegrate area of 100sq ft. To provide adequate supplies, a tender carried on 14 wheels was needed, with accommodation for 18,000 gallons of water and 41 tons of coal (which nevertheless required replenishment en route). The tender weighed 188 tons fully loaded and engine and tender together totalled just short of 400 tons. Among unusual fittings, the Niagara had a 'valve pilot indicator', designed to prevent the driver from overtaxing his locomotive by indicating the maximum cut-off that could be used at any moment without causing an excessive drain on the boiler.

Remarkable work was done by the Niagara 4-8-4s during their relatively short life, but as with all other American steam power they were doomed to give way to the all-conquering diesels, and actually did so in 1945, from which time 2,000hp Electro-Motive diesel-electric locomotives in pairs took over the Twentieth Century duty. From that time onwards economies were achieved by a reduction in the cost of fuel and the abolition of the need to refuel or service the locomotives during the journey.

One other contribution to the erstwhile glamour of the Century deserves mention. Most American stations in large cities comprise a spacious entrance hall with the needed passenger facilities grouped round it, from which gates lead to platforms that are no more than passageways to the trains. New York Central's Grand Central station in New York City was no exception. From its concourse, with cathedral-like dimensions of 275ft by 120ft and 125ft high, passengers descended to a 41-track main-line station and, below that, a 39-track suburban station. But from all other main-line departures that of the Twentieth Century Limited was always distinguished. Every day a red carpet was rolled out along the entire length of its platform as a salute to its highly favoured passengers!

Below Left: Foreshadowing the doom of long-distance rail travel in North America in 1929, a Fokker passenger plane in air-rail joint service flies over the Twentieth Century Limited. Ian Allan library

Below Right: The new stock introduced to the Twentieth Century the roomette, with its own lavatory, individual heating and air-conditioning controls and fluorescent lighting. Ian Allan library

Bottom: Santa Fe commemorated the American transcontinental centennial in 1969 with this Club car finished in 1890s style for its new streamlined Kansas City Chief train. Atchison, Topeka & Santa Fe Railway

Bottom right: Latest in US commuter trains, new Budd electric rolling stock of the Long Island Rail Road, New York. Long Island Rail Road.

THE NORTH AMERICAN RAILWAY CARRIAGE

The North American railway carriage or passenger car has for many years offered the ordinary passenger standards of comfort which he will look for in vain in any other field of public transport. Before looking at the subject in more detail, a few words on its evolution will not be out of place. As in Britain, the earliest carriages on rails were but developments of the highway coach – primitive four-wheelers. The track on which they ran was often cheaply built and of light construction, and the design soon moved to a longer vehicle on two four-wheeled trucks, or bogies, which rode very much more easily. The adoption of an open (or saloon) interior, with seats on each side of a central longitudinal aisle, has been ascribed to the 'democratic' nature of American society.

As the American railroad network grew, journeys of 24 hours or more became commonplace (speeds were not high) and the need for a vehicle which made provision for both day and night travel became clear. Economy required that such a vehicle should be convertible and from a number of early designs, that of George Mortimer Pullman became most widely adopted. In the Pullman layout, groups of four seats (two facing pairs) on each side of the aisle could, by rearrangement of the cushions and backs, be made into a bed, or lower berth. An upper berth was built into the upper wall and ceiling panelling and could be lowered when required; privacy was achieved by heavy curtains. Toilet facilities were provided at the car ends.

American railways, with little traffic offering in early days, had to be cheaply built and high-level station platforms were an expensive luxury when perhaps only two or three trains a day were involved. Passenger cars were thus provided with open vestibules at each end, with steps down almost to rail level. The final gap to the ground was bridged by a portable stepping stool, placed in position during stops by a trainman.

Heating was by stove, one or sometimes two to a car, and using wood, coal or occasionally oil as a fuel. Lighting developed from oil, through gas to electricity. Seats in ordinary coaches were often reversible ('walkover') and plush finished, although rattan was sometimes used for shorter journeys. Windows generally were narrow and could be opened upwards, to admit (in summer) a cooling draught – and dust and cinders! Sometimes, a gauze sash was fitted in an attempt to reduce inblown rubbish, and in the northerly areas, a second glazed window, or storm sash, could be fitted in winter. Early and widespread adoption of the clerestory roof contributed both to ventilation and to lighting; it continued to feature in new construction up to about 1930.

The early car bodies were mainly of wood construction but increasing size of vehicles and emphasis on greater safety led first, in the latter part of the 19th century, to the steel underframe and eventually, in late Edwardian times, to the all-steel car.

As car design developed, meeting the needs of an expanding, prosperous nation, details improved. The open-end platform gave way first to narrow enclosed vestibules, and later to full-width vestibules. Even in later years, with the very few high-level station platforms, it was necessary to provide specially for access from rail level. Doors were invariably at car ends and, outside the trucks, opened inwards. Often they were split, Dutch style, and a hinged flap (with handrail on its underside) lifted to reveal the steps.

A feature of American rail travel (to European eyes) is the door opening ceremony performed by trainmen, who also assist passengers joining or alighting from trains. Both halves of the door are swung inwards while the train is slowing, the trap is lifted and clipped up, the handrail is wiped clean of dust with a paper towel after the trainman has descended to the bottom step, with the stepping stool ready, and finally, as the train stops, the stool is placed on the ground beside the steps.

By late Victorian times, a considerable degree of comfort was provided. Dining cars had replaced station meal stops, so reducing journey time, and both dining and sleeping cars were ornately decorated, in keeping with the times, with a high degree of craftsmanship used in decorative woodwork of various styles. Electric light was coming into use, and the Westinghouse air brake, adopted earlier, improved not only safety but comfort in

stopping. Car lengths had increased from the early 50 or 60ft to 70 to 75ft. The larger and heavier cars often rode on two 6-wheeled bogies, which became universal for Pullman's sleepers and dining cars.

The ornate finish was not confined to interiors. Externally, dark green was, perhaps, the most common livery, and 'tuscan' red was used by a number of companies, including, up to the last few years, the Pennsylvania, and Canadian Pacific. The railway's name appeared along the 'letter board' above the windows, commonly in gold leaf and usually in an extended Roman script, with serifs. Car sides prior to adoption of the all-steel body were often matchboarded and could be elaborately lined out, though the last-named feature became a casualty of the 1914-18 war.

With the larger cars, windows of passenger spaces were often arched, with the upper part fitted with stained glass. An essential feature of all American passenger cars (in contrast with British practice) was the

the all-steel car. Initially, constructional details continued to give a visual impression of the later ornate styles of the wooden car. After the 1914-18 war (during which American railways were placed under government control), designs were much simplified; while there was no diminution in comfort, ornate decoration was largely cast aside. In its place came simplicity and standardisation.

This is an appropriate place to make the point that few American railroads had or have sufficient capacity to build all their own rolling stock (or, for that matter, locomotives). There is a very sizeable industry in the USA manufacturing both freight and passenger vehicles and while some railroads' railway works ('backshops') could, and did, manufacture locomotives or cars (the Pennsylvania built both at its Altoona, Pa, shops), outside purchase was more common.

Interworking in traffic had long made some degree of standardisation essential, and purchasing from common

handbrake. On open-platform cars, it was applied by a horizontal wheel, but later, vertical wheels or levers with ratchets were provided inside the vestibule. Even after automatic brakes became universal, the handbrake was, and still is, required for parking. Another universal feature from quite early days was the provision of a supply of drinking water, sometimes iced in summer, in all passenger cars.

Two classes of travel were generally provided, 'coach', that is day-coach, with sitting accommodation for day (and night) use. First class carried a different connotation from Europe. A first-class ticket entitled one to occupy Pullman car sleeping space, which had to be paid for additionally, but there was no ordinary first-class accommodation. First-class day travel could be either in a Parlor car, where a seat supplement was payable, as in a Pullman car in Britain, or by day occupancy (if the train times and journey permitted) of sleeping-car space. 'Pullman' and 'sleeper' are almost synonymous in American practice.

The Parlor car, provided where day-time demand for first-class travel warranted it, was arranged with single armchairs each side of a central longitudinal aisle; it carried a Pullman porter to serve light refreshments from a pantry or small buffet. Each sleeping car had its own attendant, or porter, traditionally a negro, who stayed with the car for each journey. (He would sleep in an unoccupied berth when available; otherwise he made do in his cubicle seat, or in the smoking room at the car end).

The Edwardian period witnessed the development of

equipment manufacturers carried the process considerably farther, so that the 1920s became known as the Standard Era.

Use of Pullman cars was particularly influential, for the Pullman Company provided sleeping car service under contract to almost every road which required it. The Pullman fleet rose to almost 10,000 cars by 1931, and 4,000 of them were of one basic design. That was the 12-1 type; it contained 12 sections, each with lower and upper berths, plus a drawing room for three persons with its own toilet cubicle.

For the 24 possible occupants of the sections, separate men's ('smoking') and women's ('rest') rooms were provided at opposite ends of the car. Each washroom contained two or three wash-basins, a dental bowl, a sofa or lounge chairs for three, and a single WC annexe. Towards the end of a night's journey, these facilities sometimes became heavily taxed.

The day coach, too, might well have smoking/rest room facilities at each end, but the interior was changed only in details of the fittings; seats were still arranged in pairs on each side of the central aisle. Whereas Pullman sleepers had for years been a product of the Pullman-Standard Manufacturing Company, there were other manufacturers of coach and other passenger vehicles; American Car & Foundry was one such, with several plants, including some taken over from previously independent firms. The heavy steel 'Standard' cars weighed 80 tons, or more, and largely rode on six-wheeled trucks. A solid train of such vehicles was an impressive sight, and no mean load for the motive power → then steam, except for a few electrified sections of line.

Opposite Page (Right): Budd diesel railcar of the Dominion Atlantic Railway (constituent of CP Rail) in August 1966. J K Haywood

Opposite Page (Left): Great Northern dormitory and lunch-counter car with the fancy name 'Coer d'Alene Lake' at Whitefish, Mont, in July 1970. V Goldberg

This Page Top: Typical between-the-wars heavyweight passenger coach of Canadian National Railways, interesting in this picture for having an up-to-the-minute ACI (automatic car identification) colour code on its side. J R Batts

Right: Observation dome car on Norfolk & Western Railway City of St Louis train in August 1961. J K Hayward

Below: Denver & Rio Grande Western Railroad traditional (1880) narrow-gauge clerestory-roof coaches, much rebuilt and preserved at Silverton, Colorado, pictured in July 1970. V Goldberg

It is worth looking at the make-up ('consist') of a typical train of the Standard Era. Behind the locomotive came the headend cars. Leading them would probably be a Railway Post Office car (RPO) carrying mail and with sorting facilities for en route dropping and collection. Behind the RPO would be baggage and express cars, for passengers' luggage and parcels traffic. Baggagemen, express messengers, and postal clerks — the latter two categories often armed with revolvers — had their duties 'up front'.

Next came the coaches; often one would be set aside for local passengers making short journeys, while passengers for major stations might be directed to particular coaches, thus making on-train ticket checking somewhat easier. Between the coaches and the Pullmans came the dining car, kitchen section to rear (so that the train's draught did not blow the heat from the kitchen back on to the diners). Then came the Pullmans and, at the rear of any train worth its salt in the nineteen-twenties, an observation car, at one time with the traditional open rear-end platform and brass railings, but later more likely a solarium or enclosed lounge space with large windows. Although Pullmans were convertible for day use, passengers could also sit in the lounge (and, except during the period of Prohibition, enjoy a drink). The lounge car might also have certain other on-train facilities, maybe a library, or a barber shop (with shower), or even a radio.

A long-distance through train of the period might run over the tracks of two or three companies, each of which contributed cars for the train, in proportion to their part of the mileage. Often, in such cases, the regular cars for the train would carry the name of the train on the letter board instead of the company owning the car. With many journeys over 24 hours, several sets of trains were often needed to meet the requirements of a particular service in each direction. Such, then, was railway travel in the Standard Era.

The spread of paved roads and use of private motor-cars, the practical development of commercial flying and the depression, from 1930 made heavy inroads into rail passenger business. Contraction was severe, but several developments in the early 1930s brought the internal-combustion engine to main-line passenger service, in conjunction with new lightweight highspeed motorised trains, albeit of rather limited capacity. The Budd Company of Philadelphia pioneered the production of a much lighter type of locomotive-hauled passenger car. It had load-bearing sides of welded corrugated stainless steel. Gone were the rivetted sides and clerestory roof, replaced by a sleek bright car, 85ft long, with large 'picture' windows, riding once again on two four-wheeled trucks. Weight came down to around 60 tons, despite the fitting of air conditioning, reclining seats, electric ice water coolers and so on.

Air conditioning was also applied, in the nineteen thirties, to existing Standard cars, firstly to diners, then to sleepers, and to a limited extent, to coaches. The financial position of many railways after the depression restricted investment in new stock, hence the refurbishing of older cars, which had then to meet the enormous flood of war-time traffic, without benefit of new construction, while builders were on war production work.

After the war, large orders were placed for passenger cars and in the period from about 1946 to 1957, the principal trains, and many others, on the majority of railroads were re-equipped with entirely new sets of cars. Some lines favoured the stainless-steel finish, others adopted smooth-sided lightweight cars, with distinctive colour schemes. To re-equip a transcontinental train running from Chicago to the Pacific coast might require five or six trains-sets with up to 18 vehicles in each; an expensive investment.

The Pullman car changed greatly in the 'streamline' era. The demand was now for accommodation with more privacy. The roomette, with a fold-away bed, was in fact a single room with built-in toilet facilities. Bedrooms and compartments each provided space for two, and drawing rooms for three people. All except roomettes could be obtained *en-suite,* for family use by folding away the common dividing partition.

Each of the vehicle types mentioned earlier was represented in streamline form, although the observation car took on a round-ended rear lounge. The most distinctive new post-war innovation was the Dome car. Used mainly in the west, where clearances were adequate, the vista-dome provided glazing not only at each side, but ahead, to the rear and in the roof. It was an instant success on scenic routes. Generally, a dome was associated with a coach (second-class) configuration, with generously spaced reclining seats at normal floor level and washrooms located beneath the dome. Dome sleepers, and dome-cafe cars were also built, and today, AMTRAK, the US Government corporation which operates most long-distance passenger trains, includes dome equipment on most of its services, except in the east where clearances are tighter.

AMTRAK today operates its nationwide services with the best of the streamline equipment. Let us hope that these most comfortable of public transport vehicles continue to make it possible to enjoy 'riding the rails' long into the jet-plane era.

Right: Super-dome car of Milwaukee Road's Morning Hiawatha train. J K Hayward

SUPER TRAINS AND FLORIDA SPECIALS

Zephyrs and Hiawathas, Chiefs and Rockets, Daylights and 400s, Florida Specials and countless Limiteds – all household names in America in the nineteen-thirties, -forties and -fifties. Each such title, with an appropriate prefix, denoted some crack passenger train, sometimes involving more than one railroad. Space allows us to consider here only three groups of these crack streamlined trains.

Pride of place, and hence first mention, must go to the Zephyrs. It comprised a three-car train set, articulated throughout, and carried on four trucks (bogies). The leading vehicle was a 600hp locomotive whose power unit was a Winton 201A diesel engine mounted integrally with the bogie. Weighing under 100 tons, the three-car train carried just 72 passengers in its two trailer cars. The car bodies were of fluted stainless-steel construction and were built by the Budd Company in Philadelphia. The train was given the name Pioneer Zephyr. It was built early in 1934 and displayed in Chicago at the Century of Progress Exposition that year.

After a series of demonstration runs, towards the end of 1934 the train entered revenue-earning service between Kansas City, Omaha, and Lincoln, Nebraska, a run of 250 miles. A similar train set, but with a coach (second-class) seat section (instead of baggage space) in the rear end of the leading (power) car, went into service between Boston and Portland, Maine, in 1935 for the

Boston & Maine and Maine Central railroads. That one was named Flying Yankee; it is now preserved at Edaville, about 40 miles from Boston. The Pioneer Zephyr is also preserved, at the Chicago Museum of Science & Industry.

The Pioneer Zephyr was followed in 1935 by three more train sets. The first two, still of three cars each, seated 88 and entered service as Twin Zephyrs in April between Chicago and the Twin Cities (St Paul and Minneapolis), taking 6½ hours for the 437-mile journey. Their route was markedly longer than the two alternatives, those of the Milwaukee Road (421 miles) and of the Chicago & North Western Railway (407 miles). The Third new train was of four passenger cars, seating 92, and an additional baggage/mail car. It became the Mark Twain Zephyr, running between St Louis and Burlington, Iowa, 221 miles, in 5¾ hours with a number of stops. Later, from 1941, this route was also covered by the Zephyr-Rocket, an overnight train between St Louis, Burlington and Minneapolis, using Rock Island tracks north of Burlington on the 585 mile run to the Twin Cities, a 14 hour journey.

More Zephyrs appeared towards the end of 1936, when two 1,800hp locomotive units, named *Pegasus* and *Zephyrus*, entered service on the Chicago-Twin Cities run, with seven-car trains, each set making a round trip

daily. The original Twin Zephyr three-car trains were found new fields elsewhere on the Burlington system. One became the Sam Houston Zephyr, running the 283 miles between Fort Worth, Dallas and Houston in five hours. The other set became the Ozark State Zephyr, between St Louis and Kansas City (279 miles).

Also in 1936 came the two train sets which formed the original Denver Zephyrs. Each partly articulated train was hauled by a two-unit locomotive totalling 3,000hp. The pairs of locomotives were named, *Silver King/Silver Queen* and *Silver Knight/Silver Princess*, respectively. Each of the 12-car trains included coaches, a dining car, four sleepers and an observation car, as well as a crew dormitory/Passenger lounge car and a combined power generator/Postal/baggage car. The Denver Zephyrs unquestionably provided facilities which set standards for 20 years or more, including such novelties as tightlock couplers, double glazing, foam rubber seats and electric razor power points. The passenger cars were named, using the common prefix Silver — because of the unpainted stainless-steel outer panelling, which was to become a familiar feature of many streamlined trains in years to come. The trains entered daily overnight service with an exciting 16-hour schedule for the 1,034-mile Chicago-Denver run.

In 1939, the 1000hp locomotive *Silver Charger*, the last to be styled in similar fashion to the Pioneer Zephyr (as were all those mentioned so far) entered service with the General Pershing Zephyr on the St Louis-Kansas City run. There are two other pre-war Zephyrs still to be mentioned, the Silver Streak Zephyr between Kansas City and Lincoln (the route of the Pioneer Zephyr) and, later in the year, the Texas Zephyr, running 834 miles, between Denver and Dallas over the Colorado & Southern lines. Not all of the Zephyrs introduced after the 1936 train sets were wholly of stainless steel. Some trains included refurbished sleeping cars of earlier heavyweight pattern.

Eventually the earliest of the epochmaking diesel trains became outdated; by 1942 the Pioneer Zephyr had moved to the secondary Lincoln-Hastings-McCook service, making local stops over part of the Denver Zephyr route. The Chicago Burlington & Quincy RR was first to introduce the now familiar-Vistadome coach, in 1947, in what might be termed the third generation of twin-Zephyr trains. The 1936 train sets so displaced from the Twin Cities run moved to the eastern half of the Chicago-Denver route, providing fast daytime service between Chicago, Omaha and Lincoln, about 557 miles, taking about 11 hours for the run with about 20 stops.

The high point of the Zephyr era came, many observers feel, in 1949 with the introduction of the California Zephyr. This train, often with five dome cars in its formation, ran between Chicago and Oakland (for San Francisco), about 2,525 miles. As far as Denver, Burlington tracks were used. West of Denver the spectacular Moffat tunnel route of the Denver & Rio Grande Western RR was followed, up through the front range of the Rockies and then west via Western Pacific RR across Utah and Nevada and down the scenic Feather River canyon to Sacramento and on to Oakland. Whereas the other Zephyrs had combined speed and comfort, the schedule of the California Zephyr was arranged so that in each direction, the two most scenic sections were traversed in daylight on the two days and two nights of

Milwaukee Road Olympian Hiawatha at Deer Lodge, Montana, hauled by electric loco E20 'Little Joe' in 1952. The engine was built by GE for Russia under Lease-lend, but not sent and was reduced to standard gauge for the Milwaukee company.
J M Jarvis

Above: Union Pacific's first streamlined diesel train of its named City series.
Union Pacific Railroad

the run. For years, the train ran completely filled day after day, but rising cost, rather than declining patronage, caused its discontinuance in 1970.

In the early nineteen-fifties still more Zephyrs were introduced, including a new daytime Chicago-Kansas City train (466 miles), the Kansas City Zephyr. It had an overnight counterpart in the American Royal Zephyr. The Ak-Sar-Ben Zephyr (Nebraska spelled backwards) gave overnight service on the Chicago-Omaha-Lincoln run; it received new rolling stock in the early 'fifties. The ultimate Zephyr train sets came in 1956 when two superlative 14-car trains were introduced on the trunk Chicago-Denver route; they displaced the two trains built in 1936, which were then moved to the Texas Zephyr route and the new trains took up the title of Denver Zephyr. Each of the new train sets included three dome cars, one a coach, one a buffet car, and at the rear a dome-lounge for first-class (sleeper) passengers. Each train set also included two slumber-coaches, which introduced second-class enclosed sleeping berths.

All the new types of cars from the 1956 trains are now in Amtrak service, but not necessarily on the Denver Zephyr. (Amtrak is the quasi-government USA National Railroad Passenger Corporation.) The Denver Zephyr continues to run daily, and is extended, as the San Francisco Zephyr, via Cheyenne to Ogden (over the Union Pacific RR) and thence over the Southern Pacific RR to San Francisco. West of Denver, the train runs but three days a week, except in the summer season, when it runs daily.

A second daily Hiawatha service has been restored to the Chicago-Twin Cities route by Amtrak. The North Coast Hiawatha, with a morning run northbound, is extended three days a week west from Minneapolis over the former Northern Pacific route of Burlington Northern & Seattle. The afternoon train, now named Empire Builder east of Minneapolis, (as well as over its run west to Seattle over the former Great Northern route) takes seven hours 40 minutes for the Chicago-Minneapolis run, with four fewer stops. There are corresponding runs into Chicago.

An interesting feature of the various Hiawatha trains was that the great majority of passenger cars were built in the railroad's own shops in Milwaukee, which was unusual for American railways. Exceptions to the home-building were the Super Domes, which came from Pullman-Standard. They were built in 1952 and the 10 vehicles, numbered 50-59, were among the heaviest streamlined cars ever built, weighing over 100 short tons. Because of the large glazed area, extra air conditioning capacity had to be installed. Each car had 68 seats in the dome and there were seats for a further 28 in a cafe/lounge below. Six of the Super Domes were sold to Canadian National in 1964-65 and are now in use on the Supercontinental between Edmonton and Vancouver.

The Super Domes were built for the short-lived Olympian Hiawatha service, for which Pullman-Standard also built the Skytop lounge cars; they had eight bedrooms and a glazed 21-seat lounge observation area, which formed the tail-end of the train. Pullman-Standard also built 10 sleeping cars, each with 10 roomettes and six bedrooms. They, and the Skytops, dated from 1948. All the Skytop lounge cars were sold to Canadian National in 1964, as were five of the sleeping cars in 1967. All the Pullman-built cars lacked the wood finish which was a feature of the railway-built cars; the latter were somewhat lighter in weight than contemporary contractor-built cars and it is significant that none have been purchased by Amtrak.

Under Amtrak auspices, trains between Chicago and the two northern transcontinental rail routes of Burlington Northern (the ex-GN and ex-NP lines) run over Milwaukee Road tracks as far as the Twin Cities, rather than using the traditional Burlington Route (CB & Q) via La Crosse. Apart from the shorter mileage, the present route provides the city of Milwaukee (population 750,000) with through rail service, whereas the Burlington Route lacks any major intermediate centre of population.

The modern re-routeing had a parallel in 1955. Prior to October 30, 1955, the great fleet of Union Pacific streamlined trains ran between Chicago and Omaha over Chicago & North Western Railway tracks, but from that date, UP passenger trains used the Milwaukee Road for access to Chicago. The change brought company to the Midwest Hiawatha on its Chicago-Omaha journeys. It also resulted in a change of livery for the Hiawathas; the maroon, grey and orange colours, which had undergone several variations in application over the years, were dropped in favour of UP yellow, for Milwaukee Road passenger cars were included in through services over the UP to the several Pacific coast destinations.

In addition to the four Class A Atlantics, and the six Class F7 Hudsons built for the principal Hiawatha services, half-a-dozen older steam locomotives were rebuilt with streamlined shrouds for use on lesser services. Two 4-6-0s, Nos 10 and 11 of Class G — quite small engines of 94 short tons each, were so modified for the North Woods Hiawathas in 1936 and 1937 respectively. In their new guise, they resembled the Class A Atlantics. Four 4-6-2s were modified as well, but their new styling was more akin to the Class F7 Hudson. Class F2 Pacifics Nos 801 and 812 were altered (from Class F5) for service on the Sioux Falls section of the Midwest Hiawathas; the main train was in the hands of Class A

Atlantics from inauguration at the end of 1940 to 1946-47, when diesels began to take over; the Class F5 Pacifics were finally withdrawn in 1950.

Two Class F1 Pacifics, Nos 151 and 152, were allocated to the Chippewa-Hiawatha north of Milwaukee (the train originated in Chicago). The Chip, as it was known, followed the west shore of Lake Michigan for much of its run. Its ultimate terminal was Ontonagon, on the south shore of Lake Superior. From its inauguration in 1937, Nos 151 and 152 were specially painted in Hiawatha colours, and in 1941 they were streamlined, becoming similar in appearance to Nos 801 and 812. Both were withdrawn in 1954, although the Chip was being hauled by diesel by the end of 1950, and finally discontinued running early in 1960.

In sharp contrast to the Hiawatha service to northwestern parts of the USA, the Florida Special was one of a number of trains which linked the winter resorts of Florida with New York (and many other northern cities which had chilly winters). The train had its origins in 1888 as the New York and Florida Special with a first-class-only consist making the 1,074-mile run from New York to Jacksonville in 30 hours. The train was routed over the Pennsylvania RR to Washington, thence via the Richmond Fredericksburg & Potomac RR to Richmond, and the Atlantic Coast Line RR to Jacksonville, and finally over the Florida East Coast Railway to St Augustine.

Top: The original diesel Burlington Pioneer Zephyr of 1934, as preserved at the Chicago Museum of Science and Industry. J K Hayward

Bottom: The CB & Q Denver Zephyr leaving Chicago in mid-1952. J M Jarvis

Below: A streamlined Hudson of Milwaukee Road fresh out of the shops in August 1938 to take on a Hiawatha service. J M Jarvis

The new train ran three times a week in each direction. Initially, each train set had but six cars; the baggage-dynamo car was followed by a combination smoker, a dining car and three sleepers. All 12 cars were newly built in Chicago by the Pullman Company and featured electric light, steam (not stove) heating, and vestibules throughout. The run started in Jersey City, for New York's Penn station was still two decades in the future. For its first two years, the train terminated at Jacksonville and passengers took a ferry across the St Johns River, until the latter was bridged in 1890. Its operation was limited to the winter season.

The success of the train resulted in the thrice-weekly service becoming daily, and in 1912 the train was extended to Key West, on the island-hopping line south of Miami. New equipment was assigned to the train over the years, and in the early 1920s it was renamed, more succinctly, the Florida Special, and was thoroughly modernised. Despite the depression, the train's popularity was sustained, so much so that during the 1939-40 winter season, it ran regularly in three sections each day. Penn station in New York had by then long been its northern terminal, and the running time to Miami was 26¼ hours for the 1,388 miles.

Operation of the Florida Special luxury service was discontinued during the 1939-45 war but it was reinstated after the war. In 1949, a further 65 minutes was cut from the schedule to Miami, with new lightweight streamlined stainless-steel cars and diesel traction. It was a first-class-only train, exclusively with enclosed sleeping quarters in its 12 Pullman cars and two bedroom/lounge cars. The train was further re-equipped for its 75th anniversary during the 1962-63 season. From then, it was no longer exclusively first class, and the schedule to Miami was reduced to 24 hours.

Today, alas, the Florida Special no longer runs, but Amtrak still operates two off-season New York-Florida trains, the Silver Meteor and the Silver Star, and in addition, the Floridian from Chicago. Indeed, the tourist traffic to Florida is probably the most profitable long-distance train service in the USA. The privately run Autotrain (carrying also passengers' motor cars) adds a fourth year-round service to Northern Florida.

The late Lucius Beebe recorded, in one of his several works on American 'Varnish' (express passenger trains), dozens of named trains which served Florida over the years. Apart from the Florida Special, the Atlantic Coast Line RR took part in the operation of an all-coach streamlined train in post-war years, namely, the East Coast Champion for the second-class traffic from New York to Miami, and intermediate points. The companion West Coast Champion carried Pullman (first-class) sleepers as well as coaches (second-class) to Tampa, St Petersburg and other points on the west side of the Florida peninsula. The Atlantic Coast Line RR included a network of short railway lines which had been consolidated by one Henry B Plant, and which served much of the west coast of Florida.

On the east coast, the ACL was dependent on its connection with the Florida East Coast Railway – the relatively small but eventually very prosperous railroad of Henry M Flagler, a partner in the Standard Oil Company. Flagler was one of the very few railroaders to have a train named after him. His enterprise developed many resorts in Florida, and it was he who conceived and carried out the construction of a railway over the sea by bridging a route south of Miami from island to island, to reach Key West, where steamer connection was made with Havana, Cuba. In pre-Castro days, of course, Cuba was a winter resort for Americans. The Key West extension was closed after being severely damaged in a hurricane in 1936. It is now a road.

Mention should perhaps also be made of the Seaboard Airline Railroad. (The Airline in its name refers to straight tracks and not to aeroplane services, and the term has been in use in America for 80 years or more.) The SAL served much of the same area south of Richmond, Virginia, as the ACL, and had the additional advantage of reaching West Palm Beach and Miami over its own tracks. Its crack train was the Orange Blossom Special, at one time a daily all-Pullman run between New York and Miami. Later companions to it were the Silver Meteor, Silver Comet and Silver Star, each with coach as well as Pullman space, and stainless-steel streamliners in the years following the 1939-45 war. In the 'sixties, two major changes occurred in Florida. The Florida East Coast line ceased to handle passenger traffic, after a major strike by its employees, and the ACL and SAL Railroads merged under the new title of Seaboard Coast Line RR.

Still, Florida passenger traffic by rail survives; today, for the winter of 1972-73, Amtrak is operating, over SCL tracks, two additional trains, the Vacationer and the Champion, as well as the Silver Meteor and the Silver Star, in its New York-Florida service.

Facing Page: Inside Hiawatha's Tip Top grill bar of around the 1940s period. Chicago, Milwaukee, St Paul & Pacific Railroad Company

THE HIAWATHA

In the late 1930s passenger train services in the United States of America reached the highest level of speed and comfort in their history. Recovery from the disastrous trade slump at the beginning of that decade had been rapid; competition from motorways and air services was only just beginning to be felt; and public response to improved railway facilities had been sufficiently encouraging for the railways to lay out considerable sums on new rolling stock and motive power. The diesel invasion was then still in its infancy, so that reliance was still being placed on steam for most of the fastest passenger services in the country.

All the railways in the USA were privately owned, and in many directions were keenly in competition with each other. This applied to the services connecting Chicago with the Twin Cities of St Paul and Minneapolis, which were three in number and all roughly equal in length. They were those of the Chicago, Burlington & Quincy; the Chicago, Milwaukee, St Paul & Pacific; and the Chicago & North Western Railways. The two last-mentioned served intermediately the important

city of Milwaukee, but the fairly densely populated country between the terminals of each route also contained a number of good-sized towns at which stops helped to swell the passenger complements of the principal expresses. The Burlington route measured 427 miles in length from Chicago to St Paul; the Milwaukee line 410 miles; and the North Western, the shortest of the three, 396 miles.

Up to 1934 a journey between Chicago and St Paul or Minneapolis usually involved night travel; the one or two day trains by each route took about 10 hours. By then motorways had made 50mph road journeys possible between these cities, and road competition was beginning to cut into railway patronage. In that year both the Milwaukee and the North Western companies conducted some speed experiments over their well-aligned routes between Chicago and Milwaukee, a distance of 85 miles in each case, in preparation for acceleration.

So it was that on July 20, 1934, steam locomotive 4-6-4 No 6402 of the Milwaukee Road headed a special five-coach train of 347 tons, which covered the 85 miles in 67 minutes 35 seconds, at a start-to-stop average of 75.5mph; once clear of the speed restrictions through the suburbs of both cities, an average of 89.9mph was maintained over 68.9 miles of the journey and a maximum of 103½mph was attained — one of the fastest runs that had been made with steam power in the USA to that date. The startling result of the series of tests was the announcement that from early in 1935 all three competing routes would cut the times of their fastest trains between Chicago and the Twin Cities from 10 to 6½ hours. While the Burlington authorities decided on diesel power for their new trains, the Milwaukee for a number of reasons decided to stick to steam, as also did the North Western. The latter was content to operate with Standard equipment, but in 1934 the Milwaukee had made its high speed intentions clear by ordering from the American Locomotive Company two 4-4-2 locomotives of an entirely new type — probably the last Atlantic steam design in world railway history.

Meantime, in accordance with American practice, names had to be thought out for the new trains. The Chicago & North Western, with a route of round about 400 miles to be covered in roughly the same number of minutes, decided on Twin Cities 400, and followed up with a number of other '400s' over various main lines which had no similar 400-mile qualification. The Burlington chose the title Twin Cities Zephyr, and diesel-operated Zephyrs became a feature of Burlington operation from that time on. The Milwaukee management thought first of Flash, but a suggestion from the Mechanical Engineer's office of Hiawatha after Longfellow's legendary Indian who was fleet of foot, was the title adopted.

The new Milwaukee Atlantics, Nos 1 and 2, were delivered in May 1935. The class was oil-fired and had 7ft coupled wheels and 19in by 28in cylinders; the firegrate area was 69sq ft, heating surfaces totalled 3,245sq ft, superheating surface was 1,029sq ft and working pressure was 300lb per sq in. Locomotive weight in working order was 125 tons, of which 62½ tons was available for adhesion. The 10-wheel tenders carried 4,000 gallons of fuel oil and 13,000 gallons of water and weighed 110½ tons.

A streamlined shroud covered each locomotive, which was the more striking in appearance because of the livery chosen — a broad orange band, edged with crimson, extending from above the front pilot, or cowcatcher, round both sides of the engine to the cab, the sides of which with the tender were orange from top to bottom. The boiler casing was a light brownish grey, and round the front of the engine it carried handsome stainless steel wings, with a large number on a red ground in the centre and the standard American headlight above. Above the boiler was a black casing, which concealed the chimney and other boiler mountings. The special coaches built for the service also shared the crimson-lined orange livery.

The Hiawatha started its revenue-earning career in August 1935. It began as a six-coach formation. Next the engine came what was officially described as a restaurant buffet, which included what was probably the first cocktail bar to be introduced on an American train and also a 'Tip Top Tap' room; then came three open 'coaches' (the American equivalent of British second class), followed by a Pullman parlour car and a beaver-tailed observation car (which probably provided the inspiration for the British LNER's beaver-tail observation car on the Coronation streamliner two years later). At a later date the buffet-restaurant was transferred to a more easily accessible location in the centre of the train.

At first the Hiawatha made one trip in each direction daily. There were five intermediate stops, and the booked average speeds between them westbound were 68.0, 66.4, 71.8, 66.7, 55.2 and 59.4mph; travelling east the corresponding speeds from St Paul were 58.5, 55.2, 69.0, 73.9, 67.2 and 68.0mph. The whole journey of 410 miles, five stops included, was completed in 6½ hours in each direction, at an overall average of 63.1mph. The new Atlantics were quick to show their paces. On a test run on May 15, 1935, with a complete Hiawatha train set, No 1 covered the 136 miles from Milwaukee to New Lisbon in 115 minutes at an average of 74.9mph, reaching a top speed of 112.5mph. The new schedule, however, had contemplated a speed ceiling of only about 90mph, though speeds up to 100mph would not be frowned on if necessary for timekeeping; eventually the cant of the track on many curves was increased sufficiently to make 100mph speeds quite comfortable for passengers.

On May 29, 1935, the Hiawatha entered revenue service, and was an immediate success. Soon its patronage was exceeding that of the competing North Western 400s and Burlington Zephyrs, carrying well over 200 passengers daily; a month after its inauguration a fourth second-class coach was added, and a month later a fifth, making the train up to eight vehicles. Duplicate trains had to be run at weekends, and two more Atlantics, Nos 3 and 4, joined the first two. In its first year of operation the Hiawatha earned $700,000 clear of operating expenses, interest and depreciation. A brand new set of coaches appeared in 1936 and yet another in 1938, each more luxurious than its predecessor, and passenger patronage steadily increased; by 1936 an average of 723 passengers was being carried by the two Hiawathas daily. On October 6, 1938, in 40 months, the total number of passengers reached the million mark.

The limit load for the Atlantics on the scheduled timings had been set at nine coaches, and it became clear that with passenger patronage steadily growing, greater

locomotive power would be needed. Consequently, in September 1938 there appeared the first of a new F7 Hudson 4-6-4 class — some of the finest locomotives both in appearance and performance that ever graced American metals. The 7ft coupled wheels of the Atlantics were retained, but cylinder dimensions were increased to 23½in by 30in, firegrate area was increased to 96.5sq ft, heating surface went up to 4,166sq ft and superheating surface to 1,695sq ft. Working pressure remained at 300lb per sq in. Weight in working order of 185½ tons included 96½ tons adhesion. Coal (automatically fired) was substituted for oil as fuel and the 12-wheel tender, accommodating 25 tons of coal and 20,000 gallons of water weighed 167½ tons. In running order, therefore, engine and tender turned the scale at 353 tons.

What these remarkable machines could do on the track became almost legendary. On one journey, with a nine-coach train of 385 tons, No 100 cut the 75-minute schedule for the 85 miles from Milwaukee to Chicago to 69 minutes 27 seconds, including the necessarily rather slow running through the outskirts of Milwaukee and the suburbs into Chicago, and a 50mph slow passage through Rondout. Over practically level track 31 consecutive miles were covered at 100mph or over, with a maximum of 110mph. Another of the Hudsons was once called on in an emergency to handle two night sleeping car trains coupled together, and worked the resulting enormous 1,905-ton train from a dead start up to 70mph in no more than 12 miles of level track.

By 1939 duplications of the Hiawathas were becoming so frequent, to cope with public demand, that it was decided to run a Morning Hiawatha and an Evening Hiawatha in each direction daily. The westbound morning train was slower than the other three, as it was scheduled to make 16 regular and two conditional stops between Chicago and St Paul, and so took seven hours 50 minutes for the run, though it shared in the common 75-minute booking for the 85 miles from Chicago to Milwaukee. By January 1940 the fastest overall time

Left: Brand-new Hiawatha train posing for publicity pictures at Brookfield, Wisconsin, in 1938. 'Trains' Magazine

Right: The Baldwin-built 4-6-4 No 6402 which made the record runs on July 20, 1934. Chicago, Milwaukee, St Paul & Pacific Railroad Company

Below: Typical interior of observation coaches used on American top trains, in this case on the upper deck of a 'dome-lounge', with a bar and lounge below, used on the GNR Empire Builder. Great Northern Railway

Below right: Inside the Skytop lounge of the Hiawatha in 1948. Chicago, Milwaukee, St Paul & Pacific Railroad Company

came down to 6¼ hours for the 410 miles between Chicago and St Paul, and the eastbound Morning Hiawatha set up a new record by being booked over the 78.3 miles from Sparta to Portage in 58 minutes, to make an average of 81mph; it thus became the only train in world history that was ever scheduled at over 80mph from start to stop with steam power. Equally the Hiawathas were the only expresses ever required to run at 100mph with steam locomotives.

But the reign of the magnificent Type F7 4-6-4s was destined to be cut short. On September 20, 1941, almost three years to the day after the first F7 had headed one of the Hiawatha trains, coming events cast the first shadow over the Hudsons. It was the appearance at the head of the Morning Hiawatha at Minneapolis of two Electro-Motive diesels giving 4,000hp that heralded the ultimate takeover of all the Hiawatha services by diesel power.

By then, however, the public reaction to the speed and luxury of Hiawatha travel had become so favourable that similar trains had been introduced over other parts of the Milwaukee system. In 1936 the North Woods area of Wisconsin, which up till then had been served by connection with the Twin Cities at New Lisbon, got its own through North Woods Hiawatha between Chicago and Minocqua. The following year saw the introduction of the Chippewa Hiawatha, taking another route northward from Milwaukee, parallel to Lake Michigan and terminating at Ontonagon on Lake Superior. Next, in 1940, came the Mid-West Hiawatha, with an eight-hour run between Chicago and Omaha that boldly challenged the Chicago & North Western and the Burlington services between those cities, and carried a through portion, detached at Manilla, for Sioux City.

But more important than all of them was the Olympian Hiawatha, a through express over the 2,207 miles between Chicago and Seattle, with a through section for Tacoma, introduced in 1947. The 45-hour journey of this express required six complete 12-car trains for its daily maintenance in both directions, including, of course, various types of sleeping accommodation, and the dome observation cars that were becoming common on American long-distance trains. The Olympian was also the only Hiawatha to require electric haulage over part of its route, as the 438 miles of the main line through the Rockies between Harlowton and Avery, Montana, were electrically worked; over the remainder of the route three-unit diesels of 6,000hp were required.

Rolling stock displaced from the original Hiawatha trains by the introduction of new and still more luxurious sets were used to form various of the later services, though large numbers of new coaches also had to be built to satisfy the demand. Similarly, as the Atlantics and the Hudsons by degrees gave place to diesels between Chicago, Milwaukee, St Paul and Minneapolis, they found plenty of employment on the other Hiawatha trains, supplemented by older 4-6-2 and 4-6-0 locomotives which were dressed up for the purpose with Hiawatha colours and partial streamlining.

Needless to say, the 4,000hp diesel (later 4,500hp) locomotive groups had no difficulty in maintaining the fast Hiawatha schedules between Chicago and Milwaukee. On one run with a nine-coach load the time over the 85 miles was cut to 64½ minutes start to stop —

79.1mph average — with the 62.7 miles between Signal Tower A-68 and Tower A-5 covered in just under 39 minutes at 96.2mph average. In the later part of World War II and the years immediately following, passenger traffic was so heavy that the Twin Cities Hiawathas loaded at times to 14 or 15 coaches.

Before long, however, the decline began to set in. In the 1960s the various Hiawathas began to disappear, one of the first being the Olympian, in 1961, after a reign of no more than 14 years. A steady deceleration also set in. Today all that is left is one daily Hiawatha taking seven hours 50 minutes in each direction between Chicago and Minneapolis, compared with the former 6¾ hours, while the one-time 75-minute and 80-minute sprints over the 85 miles between Chicago and Milwaukee have given place to a minimum time of 90 minutes. Such has been the sad end of one of the finest passenger services in railway history.

Top: Hiawatha and streamlined 4-6-4 at 60mph in August 1941. C J Allen

Above: Hiawatha stock getting an outing on a Kalmbach Special. 'Trains' magazine

THE CREWLESS LOCOMOTIVE

The opulent years of passenger railroading in the United States reached a climax in 1928-29, years which are nostalgically referred to as 'those golden years'. Through the 1930s and 40s the railroads were able to muster only a lower and lower share of this business with the down-trend sharply declining after the war. With little reason to believe that the trend could be significantly altered, railroads placed highest priorities on increasing freight revenues. Engendered in the 30s this emphasis spawned such fascinating phenomena as the super Mallet and the Big Boy dual-purpose locomotives, tripleheaded steam engine operations, the unit train, centralised traffic control, the doublehump yard, and a great raft of other ideas for boosting freight ton-mileage. The railroads' flirtation with tonnage became a dramatic spectacle of unparalleled proportions, and was quite a show to witness at trackside.

In the summer of 1939, the diesel-electric road locomotive was successfully demonstrated to be much more than a mere alternative to steam for powering trains. Its high starting tractive effort and smooth response rekindled the American romance with the gross ton-mile, and the diesel's total economic superiority doomed the steam engine for ever. But the diesel had another attribute, more subtle than the others, that sparked the motive power revolution of the 40s. The diesel-electric locomotive unit could be worked in multiple.

MU is the acronym for Multiple Uniting, and means that, with certain control equipment and wiring, locomotive units can be 'plugged-in' to each other and controlled by the leading locomotive unit. The idea was not born with the diesel, having been developed for electric traction years earlier, but the hard facts were that no one had invented a way to MU steam engines during the many years they dominated the motive power scene. Using two steam engines on a train, called double-heading, required the use of a second crew; triple-heading required three crews, and so on. Apart from the additional crew cost was the problem of adequate co-ordination of the several engines to minimise drive-wheel slippage and shocks to the train while maximising utilisation of available power. Yet the increasing size of trains to be handled over the many long grades encountered often demanded these techniques be used to move the tonnage, and railroads double- and triple-powered heavy trains regularly. The diesel appeared to render the problem academic.

Locomotive builders and their customers met repeatedly to standardise the control methods which would allow one builder's diesels to MU with another's. It was obvious that, as electrical and air braking technology progressed, the number of diesels that could be grouped was virtually inlimited. A locomotive group, called a consist, could be far greater than the largest steam engine in terms of power and drawbar pull. One-station control was infinitely more practical than double- and triple-heading, and the quick-disconnect control concept added a degree of flexibility unknown to the steam engine. Moreover, diesels of different weight and power could be mixed within the same consist in building-block fashion, and consists could be tailored exactly to a specific operating need.

By the mid 1950s, US railroads began trading worn-out diesels in for new ones of higher power, needed to meet service demands for bigger and heavier trains and shorter time schedules. The piggyback and container-on-flatcar trains had become a booming business, and much revenue was to be sought with the drag (heavy and slow) freight train. And, if any single practice will distinguish the American railroad, it is surely their version of the drag freight. It is the drag freight that led American railroads first to practise double-heading steam, and then to put long consists of diesels together to pull it; and it is with the drag train that the story of the crewless locomotive begins.

It is uncertain exactly when the term 'drag' was first applied to a slow-moving freight train. When loaded down with much tonnage, a steam engine would often be seen moving along at a snail's pace, virtually struggling for each foot of track. Long strings of wagons rumbling along behind one, two, or sometimes three engines were moved at speeds as low as 5mph and gave the appearance of being dragged by the motive power. Unlike the high-value manifest trains, schedules for the drag freight were secondary; the primary objective being to move as much tonnage as possible at the least operating cost. Drag tonnage usually meant bulk shipments of medium- and high-density goods such as coal and mineral ore, lumber, petroleum, chemicals, cement, ballast and so on or, just as often, simply solid blocks of empties being returned for reloading. The drag freight was and is a long heavy train, and bears a close resemblance to a giant conveyor-belt system. The drag concept did not change when the diesel arrived, the trains just got longer and heavier.

The characteristics of the traction motors used in the diesel-electric locomotive are such that its tractive effort (drawbar pull) increases as the forward speed of the locomotive becomes less, though speed must be kept above 8-12mph to prevent overheating the motors. The full-throttle tractive effort developed by a modern four-axle diesel at minimum continuous speed exceeds 50,000lb per locomotive. It is quite true that many steam engines could also exceed this figure at the same speed, but MU rendered the diesel superior; a consist of five four-axle units, for example, with an aggregate tractive effort of 250,000lb, can handle 10,000 tons of goods on a gradient of 1 in 100, and more on level track. Steam could seldom haul such trains even if double- or triple-headed, yet 10,000- to 20,000-ton trains of 200 cars or more are dispatched regularly over today's US railroads, each train under the control of but one engine crew. The significance of MU can not be over-emphasised.

As a train leaves level track and begins to climb, its resistance to forward movement increases. This is because a part of the train weight must now be raised as well as rolled forward, overcoming the pull of gravity. The diesel (or straight electric) will lose forward speed until the increasing tractive effort it is producing balances the effort required to pull and lift the train. It follows, then, that the maximum amount of trailing tonnage a diesel consist can pull up a grade will be something less than the maximum amount the same consist can pull on level track. This physical relationship led the railroads to develop the 'ruling grade' method of locomotive assignment, a method that ensures adequate power for a given train for climbing the steepest grade on the run. Ruling grade train rating has several limitations, however, depending upon the length and rise of the grade to be encountered. Powering a train to make the grade may lead to assignment of redundant power when operating over the level portions of the run. Also, there is a limit based upon the physical strength of the couplers of the first few cars as to how much pull a train can sustain during grade operations. Either of these limitations must be evaluated from the standpoint of some alternative method for attacking the ruling grade.

One such alternative is to 'double' the grade, meaning to take the train up the grade in sections, and then coupling it back into a single train at the top. This allows use of only the amount of power necessary to operate over the level portions. However, much time is lost in doubling and a preferred method of handling steep grades is to use special consists of locomotives, called pushers (bankers in Britain) to help push the train up the grade. At the top, the pushers are cut away and returned downgrade for the next train. For extra-heavy trains where there is danger of buckling the train with pushers, railroads often cut a third consist of power into the train somewhere near its middle. The mid-train consist helps to push the forward portion of the train and pull the rearward portion, keeping the length of any block of wagons from exceeding a specified limit.

The use of both pushers and mid-train units is common to many railroads. At the Pennsylvania Railroad's famous Horseshoe curve near Altoona, Pa, one can witness these operations many times a day; although it is a spectacular bit of railroading to watch, pusher and mid-train operations pose a common disadvantage. As neither the pusher nor the mid-train consist can plug-in to the head-end locomotives, extra crews are required to operate them, and the problems of double- and triple-heading return. The idea of a *crewless* locomotive offered the railroads some intriguing possibilities for dealing with the situation.

There are other drag train operating problems which are alleviated, to a degree, with mid-train or pusher units. One concerns train air breaking, often a problem with the longer freight trains. Certainly a story in itself, the air brake is a marvellous and highly developed system for controlling train speed, and remains the least costly method among all alternatives. Its major deficiency is its rather sluggish response, a problem further aggravated by higher speeds and very long trains. Consider a 160-car train pulled by a locomotive consist from its head-end. The last car of the train will be over one mile from the locomotives and its sole communication with them for braking purposes is

Above: Groups of locomotives are used at the rear and mid-train positions as well as the head to lift this very heavy freight train up the 1 in 54 Allegheny grade through Horseshoe curve on the Pennsylvania line. D H Ellsworth

through a 1½-inch brake pipe. Because air is a fluid of definite mass, friction of the brake pipe interior will hamper the flow of air and the waves of pressure gradients which must be realised at each car for brakes to be operated on that car. Friction and pipe leakage can delay the initiation of brake actions on each car as distances become greater to the head-end units, increasing the time for all brakes to apply, release, and recharge. Suppose, now, that a consist of mid-train units or pushers could be put into direct electrical communication with the head-end so that brake actions could be initiated immediately from several points in the train. The crewless locomotive might provide the answer to the question of how to make several small trains out of one large one and still retain the single entity for one-crew operation.

A third operating problem should be brought to light, as it can be considered the most serious one challenging the long freight train. It deals with an elusive railroad item known as 'train slack'. Slack aptly describes the free play between coupled railroad cars, and this free play is additive as the length of a train increases. When no slack exists between cars, the train is said to have its slack bunched. When the same train is stretched, a run-out of slack, its length might have increased by as much as one foot per car — 150 feet or more for a train of as many cars! Locomotive enginemen readily admit that the control of slack action is their toughest assignment. Out of control, slack action can become so violent that cars are buckled and crushed, trains broken in two, and the track structure under a train totally destroyed. It takes no small amount of care and skill to keep a tight reign on slack for *any* train.

The group of three pushers at rear of train on Horseshoe curve pictured on previous page. D H Ellsworth

The ideal way to operate a train would appear to be to keep it solid, either stretched or bunched, although the latter method is preferred since couplers can withstand more compressive than tensile forces. Yet it remains virtually impossible to achieve either mode when all power is concentrated at the head-end. Mid-train and pusher consists once again appeared to offer a solution if means could be found to place them under the complete control of the head-end station.

Armed with these plus factors, several progressive railroads and suppliers set upon the task of developing a crewless locomotive which could become the basis for remotely controlled locomotive consists for placement anywhere within a train. A few years ago, the details of this adventure would have been dubbed pure science fiction, but the TMU and the Space Radio systems, products of this task, are a matter of record.

The TMU (Train Multiple Uniter) system was developed and marketed by the General Railway Signal Company of Rochester, NY, for the remote control of locomotives. An electronic computer was installed aboard a modified locomotive and was electrically connected to a pair of strain-gauge transducers fitted to the rear coupler. As the pull of the trailing tonnage on that coupler increased, the strain-gauge signals sent to the computer would increase, and the computer would react to increase locomotive output. If the pull on the coupler relaxed, a reduced signal would cause the computer to reduce output. Conventional locomotives were coupled to the modified locomotive as needed, and were MUed by standard electrical jumper cables. The TMU system functioned only for mid-train consist applications, and the TMU consist was coupled into the middle of a train as needed. Pneumatic communication with the head-end was afforded by the brake pipe, and any pressure reductions for brake applications also served to cause the modified TMU locomotive to throttle back completely. The modified unit had to be the last or trailing unit of the TMU consist, and its on-board equipment could only sense a 'pull' requirement of the train's rear portion of cars. The system was not designed to sense a 'push' requirement for any portion of the train preceding the TMU consist, nor could the head-end crew call upon the TMU consist to assist in bunching train slack of this portion. The system *did* offer a way to reduce some of the strain and high tensile forces on the first few car couplers of the train, and a way to increase the tonnage moved by a single crew.

The Pennsylvania Railroad, the Louisville and Nashville Railroad, and a few others installed sets of TMU equipment in some motive power units for a series of trial runs. Judging from the fair number of modifications which soon followed, those first runs must have been very trying. It is not difficult to foresee a new set of problems created by the system, especially those con-

cerning the menace of train slack action and the predictable chaos facing a computer relying upon the *uniform* changes in pull on a locomotive coupler. Impacts transmitted to the strain-gauge coupler resulting from a run-out of slack would be answered by an immediate boost of locomotive power, and an almost simultaneous impact as slack regathered. Falling into a synchronous pattern, TMU in many instances actually aggravated the seriousness of slack action dynamics, degrading the situation considerably.

Power delay programming and logic were rushed in to modify the on-board computer, but the parted trains and other train delays had taken their toll. Railroads knew from the start that TMU was not designed to meet all of the parameters favouring remote control of pushers and mid-train units; TMU did not assist with brake applications or train charging, nor were the units under the control of the head-end station. Now, it seemed, TMU was getting into trouble with slack action. The final blow to the concept lurked in the shadow of several successful demonstrations of the space radio system, and further expenditure on TMU by the railroads was deemed pointless. It lived a brief but exciting life, and deserves consideration as the railroad's first bold step into space.

The supposed worth of mid-train power for improving air braking and train handling prompted both major US air brake manufacturers to become totally committed to investigations of remote control of railway locomotives. The Westinghouse Air Brake Company (WABCO) and affiliated Union Switch & Signal, introduced the RMU (Remote Multiple Uniter) in the early 1960s. The system was the first successfully to employ a radio link to pass control information between two locomotives not physically coupled together. Within a short time the Arnold Electric Company of Philadelphia, Pa (later merged with Radiation Inc, Florida) introduced the space radio system which was so similar to RMU that to describe one is to describe either. The Arnold/Radiation version was developed jointly with the New York Air Brake Company (NYABCO) and was called Locotrol, a name which soon became the catchword for both systems. By simulating the standard MU jumper cable with a two-way radio link, the controlled unit could be spotted up to two miles away from the controlling unit, and the avenue was suddenly made clear for achieving every one of the operating advantages sought with mid-train locomotive utilisation.

The electronics and hardware of the space radio system are very complex to describe, but the operating principles are quite straightforward. Basically, the idea is to transmit the control information, normally carried from unit to unit via the jumper cable, to the remote unit by electromagnetic radio carrier waves. The two-way link provides for 'answer-back' from the remote unit so that its status can be continually monitored from the head-end station. Also, as locomotive air brake equipment is self-contained for each locomotive, the equipment on the remote unit could be activated and monitored by radio bringing the remote unit totally into play by remote means. The command locomotive is established as the lead unit of the head-end consist, and locomotives so modified are given the fetching name of 'master'. As you can guess, the locomotive modified for remote control becomes the unglamorous 'slave'. Conventional units are added to either master or slave by standard jumper cables and are controlled by the respective modified unit. Thus, the complete train system becomes the master consist at the head-end, and one or more slave consists located within or at the rear of the same train.

The chain of events taking place for a simple command would go something similar to the following — the time lapse for the entire process is a mere fraction of a second:

(a) The engineman makes a control change on the master and consist such as a change in throttle position or application of the air brake. The master's logic circuits encode the action and feed it to a combination radio transmitter-receiver called a transceiver. The message becomes a transmitted radio signal.

(b) The slave located X number of cars back in the train and programmed to 'hear' only its own master receives the signal, and its logic circuits respond to decode the message and adjust the locomotive's controls according to the command. As units trailing the slave are MUed to it, they will do exactly as does the slave unit.

(c) An additional set of sensors reads the new status of the slave and a message is generated for transmission back to the master.

(d) The master receives the message from the slave and compares it to the original command. If there is exact compliance, the slave's status is displayed on the engineman's special console. If there is disagreement, the original command is again transmitted and the engineman is given an 'alert' display. Within seconds the slave will either be made to comply with the command, or the entire slave consist will be neutralised.

The significance of this breakthrough for train handling lay in the fact that the air supply of the mid-train slave consist could be fully utilised for train charging and brake releases, and the slave's brake equipment would be manipulated for brake applications. Braking commands that normally took several seconds or even minutes to reach a mid-train consist's position via the brake pipe, could now reach the same location at the speed of light. Both applications and releases could now proceed throughout the train from three locations within the train with considerable reduction in time. The icing on the cake was that the electric dynamic brakes of the slave consist were also made available to the head-end station for the first time, further to aid the driver in the handling of his train.

Superior control of train slack was another improvement to be sought with radio-controlled units by virtue of their ability to be operated by the engineman independently of the head-end consist. If he wished to tighten the slack of the train's forward portion, he merely reached over to a special console and dialled up more power on the slaves. Without changing its own status, the master would tell the slave to throttle up and advance on the head-end.

It all seemed just too good to be true as the Southern Pacific Lines, the Pennsylvania Railroad (now Penn-Central Company), the Norfolk and Western Railway, the Southern Railway System, the Santa Fe Lines, and several other railroads packed the equipment aboard some of their rolling stock. (oddly enough, both RMU and Locotrol can be installed in a modified freight car rather than having to modify an already-expensive locomotive. It is necessary to equip the car for standard electrical and pneumatic cables and hoses for passing electrical and pneumatic control information to an adjacent coupled locomotive consist.) Tests and tests

and more tests were conducted with short trains, longer trains, and some record drag trains. The Pennsylvania Railroad succeeded in moving a train of 396 loaded coal cars several hundreds of miles with a pair of Locotrol units, and the Norfolk and Western Railway went one better with the all-time US record drag train of 498 hopper cars of loaded coal. The most satisfactory and useful test trains, however, were those of 175-200 cars, and there remained little doubt in anyone's mind that radio control could do the job. The day of the fully automatic train inched closer.

Operating locomotives by radio control was not all a bed of roses. Almost immediately problems began to crop up. Perhaps the most acute irregularity came as a by-product from operating in the territory most suited to the use of mid-train units and pushers — the mountains. Most rail lines threading through some mountain range are dotted with tunnels, and radio signals seldom penetrate tunnel walls. An override system was provided which could preserve the last transmitted command on the slave during a period when radio continuity was interrupted. The engineman would select tunnel-override before the lead locomotive entered a tunnel, and a command would be sent to the slave to activate a locking circuit holding slave status to the last action command stored in its memory bank. A time delay on the slave would stick or hold the locking circuit for a time sufficient to allow both the head-end consist and the slave consist to clear the tunnel. When continuity was regained, the slave would adjust to the next command. Safety during periods of lost continuity was insured since the slave consist is connected to the train's brake pipe, and the consist would be neutralised by an emergency application of the brakes. Tunnel override offered a temporary fix for test runs, and antenna systems could be placed within tunnels for permanent correction.

Unmanned wagon containing radio and control relay equipment which avoids extensive modification of locomotives for remote control, as used by Canadian Pacific unit coal trains fitted for Locotrol. CP Rail

Other continuity problems were blamed on the apparent random loss and interference due to terrain, and proved to be more difficult to circumvent. Methods had to be developed for defining the exact locations where continuity was most often disrupted, and lineside repeaters were installed. The repeaters would boost signal strength to a degree sufficient to be heard by the slave, and proper spotting of the repeaters could, in effect, bend signals around obstructions.

There have been some problems which were relatively easy to solve such as how to prevent a slave from trying to comply with two or more masters, or how to keep a slave from running away on its own at the roundhouse because its master is being operated in the vicinity. There are the usual questions as to where to place the slave consist in a train, or how many units should be coupled into the slave consist, or even how many slave consists to employ in the same train (slaves can be made to repeat commands to other slaves).

There have also been generated some rather perplexing questions which, for the most part, remain largely unanswered; for example:

(a) With the capability, now, for operating 200-300-car freight trains, what do you do with such a train when it arrives at a clogged railyard, or at a yard built years ago when trains were less than 100 cars in length?

(b) What are the responsibilities of the company and employees concerning the operation of more than one consist of locomotives by a single engineman in the same train?

(c) What are the most economical modes of operation for this expensive and sophisticated equipment?

The ramifications for total automation of railroad trains from these remote-control experiments, however, are far too great for railroads to allow testing to be discontinued. The Southern Railway System, beyond testing, put 50 sets of radio units into operation in both heavy drag and high-speed manifest services, recognising the improvement in train handling and control, and established a full service of multi-consist trains. Other major US roads, including the Southern Pacific Lines, the Penn-Central Railroad, the Chesapeake & Ohio/Baltimore & Ohio Railroads, the Norfolk & Western Railway, the Santa Fe Lines, and in Canada the Canadian National and the Canadian Pacific Railways, continue to explore radio-controlled locomotives. Computer systems and software are currently being developed for on-board computers which can read the actions of a train and select the optimum status of the locomotive consist required to control speed, slack and dynamic reactions.

The totally automated railroad is now a reality in several countries; examples include the Lindenwald commuter railroad of New Jersey, and the Muskingham coal railroad operation near Zanesville, Ohio, with at least a dozen more automated systems for the US alone planned for the coming months. Perhaps, some day, it will be said that TMU, RMU, and Locotrol, and the handful of bold men determined to make them work, were part of what progressive railroading was all about.

Right: A section of Santa Fe's electronic classification yard at Kansas City, which was a pioneer user of KarTrak ACI. Santa Fe Railway

Below: Control room of the electronic yard on the Canadian Pacific system at Alyth. CP Rail

AUTOMATIC WAGON IDENTIFICATION

Keeping records of the day-to-day movements and whereabouts of more than two million freight wagons or cars rolling constantly over 255,000 miles of North American railroad tracks is probably the industry's biggest single chore in paperwork. As every train enters or leaves each classification yard or passes through interchanges or junctions between connecting railroads, its wagons must be observed and the owner's reporting mark initials and serial numbers accurately listed. The job has always been a pencil-and-paper manual task performed by a yard clerk, car checker or 'mudhop' as he has been nicknamed. In order to secure completely accurate data, train speed past the observation points must not exceed 15mph. Occasionally, a mudhop who was endowed with a photographic memory came along; he could observe a 100-car train without writing anything, then go into the yard office and re-run the entire consist through his mind from memory, but this highly unusual breed of man was few and far between.

Once recorded and inside the yard office, car movement data through the years has undergone vast speed-ups and improved handling methods. Telegraph messages eventually gave way to telephone and teletype systems and even micro-wave transmission conducted by computer memory banks. But the only forward step in the basic old-fashioned manual gathering of wagon data has been the introduction of closed-circuit television monitors which permit the clerk at his desk, and at any distant point in the yard, to see and transmit the information to message lines or computers.

Now, through the wonders of electronics, every piece of rolling equipment from locomotives to cars to cabooses (and even piggyback road vehicles and containers) can be identified and recorded automatically as they pass a trackside equipment installation at any speed up to 80mph. Known as Automatic Car Identification (ACI), the unique system was developed in 1967-68 by the Sylvania Division of General Telephone & Electronics Corporation, Bedford, Massachusetts, who worked in collaboration with the Association of American Railroads Research Center located at the Illinois Institute of Technology in Chicago. ACI in thorough tests has proved workable and highly accurate and is today fully operational and available to all railroads.

The basic Sylvania ACI system, named Kar Trak 800 Series, consists of three major assemblies: the label, the scanner and the decoder. The colour-coded label, which obviously must appear on the sides of each wagon and piggyback vehicle, consists of 13 small stripes or

modules in single colours, or combinations of black, blue, red and white, arranged in proper sequence to identify the vehicle. The scanner reads the identifying label information from the moving vehicle. The scanner, an electro-optical device, installed at the trackside, converts the colour-coded data on the label into electrical analogue signals which are sent to the decoder. The decoder analyses and interprets the analogue signals and converts them into digital outputs for use in railroad communication, data processing and control systems.

The decoder in the basic system can be designed to work directly through various standard communications systems. However, as most of the communications systems transmit data at speeds of only between 60 and 150 words per minute, a message-storing buffer is necessary sometimes to balance a fast generation of ACI data against the slower transmission rate.

The basic ACI scanner/decoder installation can be made to perform other useful functions with the addition of various optional devices. Since all scanner readings obtained from labels are expressed in numbers, the optional Carrier Index converts each wagon owner's code number into the reporting mark initials; code number 022, for example, would automatically come out ATSF for Atchison, Topeka & Santa Fe Railway. There are several optional choices of data storing equipment which permit later delivery upon command, such as a controlling computer in the Santa Fe's Argentine (Kansas) yard which periodically polls 10 scanner/decoder sites for train movement data. There are also optional Message and Calendar devices which provide a topical heading for each train scan. Details included here are direction of train travel, scanning location, date and time. And finally, the optional Piggyback Format will scan each flat wagon and the labelled trailers or containers as well.

The success of the ACI project depends upon four million labels affixed to two million freight cars. To achieve desired results, the labels must be almost as carefully engineered as the delicate equipment that monitors them. In completed form with black borders, there are two sizes of label with colour-coded modules affixed thereon with adhesives. Modules, developed by the 3M Company of Minneapolis, Minnesota, are made from adhesive-backed retro-reflective sheeting similar to that used in road signs. Light striking the material is reflected back to its source along the path it followed when transmitted. In ordinary mirror reflection light is reflected at an angle opposite to that from which it came, or away from its source, except when mirror and light source are perpendicularly opposed. However, a retro-reflective surface reflects light back to its source regardless of the light's incoming angle. The module surface is coated with tiny glass beads, 90,000 of them per square inch, each of which is its own optical system. En masse, they reflect back to the wayside scanner light claimed to be 200 times more intense than normal reflected light from any painted or coloured object.

There are 12 different colour-coded module forms, each divided into two parts and each denoting a single number value from zero to nine, plus one for Start and one for Stop/10. The colour code is as follows and a typical label is shown in an accompanying illustration.

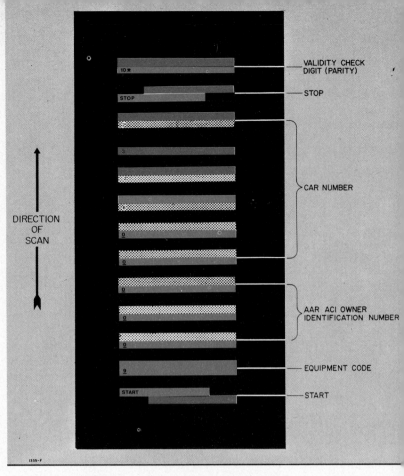

0 – Blue/White	6 – White/Blue
1 – White/White	7 – Red/White
2 – White/Red	8 – White/Black
3 – Red/Black	9 – Blue/Blue
4 – Red/Red	10/Stop – Blue/Red
5 – Blue/Blue	Start – Red/Blue

For easy identification when attaching the modules to vehicles, man-readable numbers appear on them. Each completed label must be a custom-assembled group of 13 modules to show the individual identity of each vehicle, the modules being arranged in ladder style, one above the other, to be read from bottom to top. A complete label may be assembled directly on the surface of a steel vehicle after properly preparing the area, or applied to a backing plate of steel, anodised aluminium or vinyl film for attaching to vehicles of aluminium, stainless steel or wood construction. Properly applied modules are said to perform satisfactorily in all weather conditions between temperatures ranging from minus 60 degrees F to plus 125 degrees F.

Reading from bottom to top, the general label format of 13 modules comprises: Start (1 module), equipment code number (1 module), owner code number (3 modules), vehicle serial number (6 modules), stop (1 module) and validity check (1 module). Where the owner code number is less than three digits and where the serial number is less than six digits, zero modules are inserted preceding the number in each case to bring it up to the required label spaces. Equipment code number identifies the type of rolling stock numbers running 0 for railroad and 1 for privately owned wagons, 2 to 5 for trailers and containers, 6 for works equipment, 7 for

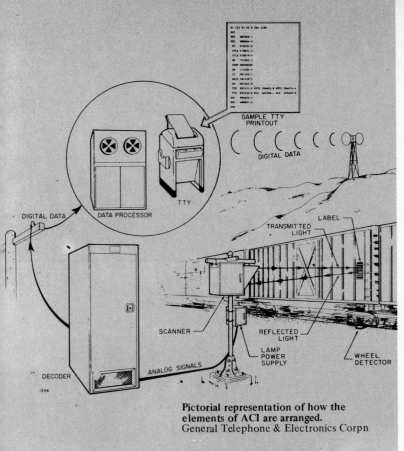

91 123 01 02 R 264 1330
ACI
WPC   083269-1
WPC   388094-4
PC   018191-5
UTLX 078891-1
UTLX 078879-4
NP   721043-5
PGBR 000000000
GM   174394-5
IC   003105-1
4632 081198-2
DH   903063-8
TTX 093181-0 RTT1 204601-8 APT2 204606-4
TTX 093100-8 822 MC59NG-- 611 407619-8
RPC   896654-3
NPC   896654-3
RPC   406897-9

SAMPLE TTY PRINTOUT

DIGITAL DATA

TTY

DATA PROCESSOR

DIGITAL DATA

TRANSMITTED LIGHT

LABEL

SCANNER

REFLECTED LIGHT

LAMP POWER SUPPLY

WHEEL DETECTOR

DECODER

ANALOG SIGNALS

Pictorial representation of how the elements of ACI are arranged.
General Telephone & Electronics Corpn

Above: KarTrak scanning equipment for mounting at the trackside. B Pennypacker

passenger coaches, 8 for cabooses and 9 for locomotives. The validity check digit is the only module that can possess a value of 10 and is arrived at through a complex multiplication, addition and division of all ten modules numbers; to make it simpler for applying correct labels in the field there is a quick-calculation chart. For locomotive labelling, the first two of the six serial numbers can be used as an optional code system to identify the type of locomotive and the remaining four spaces for the locomotive number.

Proper placement and location of labels on equipment is of importance to obtain an unobstructed scanning range. Flat areas unhindered by doors, channels, railings, rivet heads or seams should be used; on the curved sides of tankers and hoppers — special separate mounting brackets are the best solution. Tops of labels must not be more than 9ft 6in above the top of rail and there is a recommended minimum height of 6ft for normal vehicles and 16 inches for flat wagons. A label is

required on each side normally and on vehicles with more than six axles there should be two labels per side.

Sylvania markets its ACI optical/electronic equipment under the registered name KarTrak. The scanner is enclosed in a sealed steel cabinet measuring 39 inches wide, 28 inches high and 16 inches deep; it weighs 160 pounds. It is mounted on a mast located about 12 feet from the track to be scanned and 7 feet above rail level of that track, permitting a vertical scanning height range from 16 inches to 9½ feet from top of rail. The scanner is designed to withstand all weather conditions between temperatures of minus 50 degrees and plus 150 degrees F and 100 per cent humidity. A scanner cabinet contains the illuminating source, scanning optics, photo detectors, cable drivers, control electronics and electric power supply. It is connected to the decoder by a cable which can have an extreme length of 1,000 feet to reach the decoder, which must be housed in an environmentally protected building.

The scanning equipment is designed to read each passing label up to four times. The equipment starts with a 9,000-watt xenon lamp, the light from which is first routed through a series of mirrors to a multi-faceted scanning wheel, each facet of which is also a mirror. Spinning at high speed, the wheel causes the light beam to move from the bottom of the scan to the top at the same light rate. The light is projected at the label and follows the same path back to a partially silvered mirror where the returned light is focused through a lens to create an image of the label. The light in the image is optically filtered at the mirror into two broad spectra defined as red and blue. Photo-multipliers change the optical signals into electrical pulses for input to the decoder.

The heart and brains of the ACI system lie in the computer-type circuitry of the decoder unit, which is contained in a steel cabinet measuring 24½ inches wide by 73 inches high by 29 inches deep. The delicate equipment must be kept inside a building where heating and air conditioning ensure a temperature of 45 to 95 degrees F and humidity in the 20-80 per cent range. The circuitry of the decoder changes electrical imput signals from the scanner into meaningful digital values for transmission as data. It also is designed to analyse incoming signals and decide whether a proper label has been scanned and accuracy requirements have been met.

As a train approaches a scanning site, a track circuit is activated, turning on the ACI equipment. (If the decoder has an optional message/calendar device, a heading is prepared for the train report to follow.) Incoming information from each scanned label is stored momentarily in a label data register. Positive and negative checks indicate whether information received in the label data register is correct or incorrect. A positive comparison sends information to the output circuitry. If a negative comparison occurs, the information in the label data register is held while additional scans are made; another negative check causes the output circuit to send a question-mark designation.

Another decoder component, an unlabelled car detector, works in conjunction with electronic wheel sensors fitted in the railway track. The sensors count the vehicles as they pass and relay a signal for each vehicle to the detector. If the signal is not cancelled by positive check signals from the other information processing circuits, the unlabelled car detector generates a series of zeros which go to the output circuits to indicate that an unidentified vehicle has passed. Such is the speed of today's computer electronics that the entire process of reading, verifying and the rest is completed in a tiny fraction of a second and that each and every label on every passing vehicle in a train, including piggyback containers and semi-trailers, is processed separately at train speeds of up to 80mph.

With the development of a workable ACI system, the Association of American Railroads adopted strict regulations governing the proper labelling of all equipment and set a target date in 1970 for completion of the job. The monumental task has taken much longer than anticipated. However, extensive field tests on many railroads began in 1969 and between October 20 and November 28 of that year, tests on the Canadian National Railways produced some enlightening results. Alongside a westbound track leading to a receiving yard near Toronto, Ontario, two Sylvania KarTrak scanner decoder units were set up to monitor simultaneously the same trains, to provide a cross-check for label reading and reporting accuracy. The results went to a teletype output in the yard office, from which the printed car lists were taken and checked manually, car by car, after each train had stopped in the yard.

One portion of the detailed test report shows that of 1,086 complete train reports, consisting of 54,165 cars, 47,650 cars had labels and 45,365 were read correctly; 2,295 were not and were termed problem labels. There were 184 labels incorrectly read, but the biggest problem was that 1,671 were dirty and/or defective. This clearly indicated the need for strict label maintenance, the repair of damaged labels and replacement of dirty ones. Sylvania also recognised the need to try and make its equipment reject fewer marginal labels. Even so, the tests suitably impressed CNR to the point of placing an initial order for ten sets of KarTrak equipment.

ACI's potential benefits to railroading lie principally in the immediate future. At the present time only a few railroads have scanning equipment, and it is being used more or less experimentally to evaluate accuracy and ways of programming system computer networks to make the best use of ACI-generated data. But with completion of the huge labelling job this year, many carriers are expected to initiate ACI programmes, just as the pioneering Santa Fe did in early 1971 with installation of ten scanner/Decoder units at Argentine yard near Kansas City, Missouri. Each decoder can store 1,000 labels and is polled regularly and automatically for this information by an IBM 360-40 computer in the bill office. The bill office is expected ultimately to be interconnected to the system message-switching complex in Topeka, Kansas, from which information is immediately available to any department dialling for it.

The *Santa Fe Magazine* in July 1971 reported that ACI accuracy is perhaps the biggest problem, but there is also the reconciliation of data when manually recorded and ACI-generated lists differ. It is this writer's opinion that clean and easily readable labels will be the key to the success of ACI and from purely casual observations of numerous dirty labels already to be seen on cars that were labelled a year or more ago, this is bound to be ACI's biggest trouble spot. Referring again to the *Santa*

Above and below: Two pictures of a huge new hump marshalling yard at North Platte, Nebraska, USA; yards of such a size make some system of ACI virtually essential.
Union Pacific Railroad Company.

Fe Magazine, other benefits of ACI are mentioned. For example, the calendar/time device records can be used by a computer to determine the arrival and leaving times of every car in a yard; thus slow movers, stragglers and overlooked cars might be pinpointed if they have not left the yard within a specified time.

The giant Penn Central system to date has installed only two ACI scanners, which are located on-line (not in yards) in remote areas for the specific purposes of monitoring eastbound unit coal trains as they pass over electronic weigh-in-motion scales. The combined car label and weight data goes direct to a billing computer in the Philadelphia accounting offices. One of the scan/weigh locations is on the main line at Denholm, near Lewistown, Pennsylvania, and the other is upstate in the Susquehanna River valley at McElhattan, near Lock Haven; each location is positioned to process coal movements coming from each of the two principal bituminous-producing areas of the state. All this amounts to the centralised and automated processing of most coal traffic, eliminating numerous individual freight stations, manual waybilling by clerks and even waybill rate figuring. It also eliminates many weigh scales and the time required for train crews and weigh clerks to weigh each wagon individually.

Seaboard Coast Line currently has three ACI scanners in use at Hamlet, North Carolina, site of the road's largest car distribution and classification yards. The scanners generate and feed car data to an IBM 1800 computer for system-wide use. Another scanner located at Rockport, Florida, monitors perishables trains moving out of Florida and relays the data northward by teletypewriter. SCL reports that, at the beginning of 1972, it had placed ACI labels upon 92.6 per cent of its 63,214 freight cars. Since some cars stay off-line for many months, running down that final 7.4 per cent is probably the hardest part of the whole labelling job and explains why it is taking so long to get them all tagged up.

Finally, the ACI principle has almost limitless uses both inside and outside railway operation. For example, the Seaboard Coast Line has tested experimentally what is termed a Flagger locomotive malfunction indicator with moveable coloured modules. Thus, a distant terminal might be warned hours in advance of mechanical trouble in a locomotive moving toward the terminal and make preparation to attend to it. Car rental companies have also expressed an interest in ACI as a means of keeping track of what vehicles arrive at garages and rental parks so they can be immediately made available to new customers. Although developed for railroad use, ACI appears to have valuable applications throughout industry.

PIGGYBACK OPERATIONS OF NORTH AMERICA

Claimed to be the world's fastest freight train, the Super C scorches along the Atchison, Topeka & Santa Fe Railway's main line at better than 75 miles an hour! Clad in blue, silver and yellow, as many as three throbbing diesel locomotive units totalling more than 10,000 horsepower head a train made up of piggyback shipments riding on 89ft-long flat cars on roller bearing-equipped wheels. The load adds up to 2,000 gross tons of steel wagons, road semi-trailing vans, wheelless container vans and cargo all dynamically balanced and suspended precisely above the two thin-ribboned steel rails as it plummets along at quite remarkable speed.

Santa Fe created Super C in 1967 as a premium-rated train to piggyback trailers and containers at passenger train speeds. Running seven days a week as train No 198 westbound and No 891 eastbound, Super C slashes 17 hours from the next-best through freight schedule over the 2,220-mile route between Chicago, Kansas City and Los Angeles. The train is due out of Chicago at nine o'clock each morning, booked on a 40-hour schedule, but capable enginemen along the way frequently manage to put 'The C' into LA several hours ahead of time. Such speed compares with the timing of the famous passenger streamliner Super Chief, which posts a best schedule of 39½ hours over the same route. For the premium-speed freight rate of $1,484, a shipper can waybill a 17½-ton trailerload via Super C whereby it will move faster than by road and cheaper than by air. Train speed must remain consistently near, and often above, the mile-a-minute mark. But the zenith in speed probably occurs in the great South-western desert country between Winslow, Arizona and Gallup, New Mexico. Along that 127.2-mile stretch of track, train 891 is scheduled to maintain a minimum overall running speed of 72.7mph.

Super C aptly demonstrates that speed and priority handling are the names of the piggyback game, where the 90ft super flat-tops average 3½ times the daily mileage of other freight wagons. Thundering over 46 American and the two principal Canadian railroads, hundreds of daily fast-scheduled freight trains move nearly two million piggyback wagonloads annually — a truly phenomenal traffic growth for a transport service that has existed for less than two decades. Numerous trains emulate Super C by catering only for trailer and container van payloads, while many other trains sandwich piggyback wagons among the conventional mixture of boxcars, gondolas, tanks and refrigerators. Probably for lack of a better word, the highly descriptive nickname 'piggyback' has enjoyed a popular persistence through the years to denote what is officially termed TOFC (Trailers On Flat Cars) and COFT (Containers On Flat Cars).

But whatever the name, it all amounts to a very convenient and economical way to pre-package, or containerise, freight. The slow and costly chore of intermediate manual transfer of less-than-wagonload (lcl) shipments between lorries and boxcars is avoided and indeed, this deficit operation caused the phasing out of most lcl freight stations during the 1950s. In their place, a railroad or its affiliated road haulage line can offer much the same service in its own trailers as TOFC traffic. Furthermore, the same TOFC marketing is applied to solicit trainers of all common carrier hauliers where the piggyback rate on hauls of 500 miles or more is ten cents or more per ton-mile cheaper than throughout road haulage.

The idea of transporting wheeled vehicles on railroad flat cars is not a new one. Way back in 1858, the Nova Scotia Railway (now part of the Canadian Pacific's Dominion Atlantic) offered the service for farmer's wagons. Numerous crude forms of piggyback appeared through the years, mostly experimental in nature, but perhaps the longest-lasting and best-remembered is the circus train with its ornately decorated wagons. The highly refined high-speed concept of TOFC of today began in 1953, when Pullman-Standard introduced the first specially designed big flat to carry trailers. The 75ft wagon apparently appealed to Southern Pacific, which later that year established the first regular TOFC run carrying semi-trailers of its affiliated lorry line, Pacific Motor Freight, between Los Angeles and San Francisco, a distance of 470 miles.

How it all works and what makes it go is completely unlike anything ever seen in railroading, from the concepts of ratemaking to the homogeneous mating of normally opposite transport forms and the physical mechanics of rail-haul accomplishment. First must come the Plan, the foundation of agreement and paperwork to make it all possible. Under five possible plans, rates and determined by who performs what service(s) and whose equipment is used, as follows:

Plan 1 — Railroad flat cars, trucker's (road haulier's) trailers. Trucker performs pick-up and delivery.

Plan 11 — Railroad flat cars, railroad trailers. Railroad performs pick-up and delivery, but variations can have it done by truckers.

Plan 111 — Railroad flat cars, private shipper's trailers. Shipper performs pick-up and delivery.

Plan 1V — Private shipper's flat cars, private shipper's trailers. Private shipper performs pick-up and delivery.

Plan V — Railroad flat cars, railroad or trucker's trailers. Either party performs a road haul at one or both ends of the rail haul.

After the plan comes the hardware, that special type of wagon equipment designed to carry vehicles that, in the purist concept, were never intended to ride the rails. Today's piggybacking wagon or flat car is longer than a Pullman and must ride like one at high speed to protect the valuable cargo. Its loading deck measures 89 feet 4 inches long and 9 feet wide, coupled length is 92 feet 8½ inches and weight is 32 tons. Running gear is two four-wheeled high-speed bogies. While earlier versions were built in 75-foot and 85-foot lengths, today's standard car just described will accommodate one 45-foot and one 40-foot trailer, or two 40-foot trailers, or three 27-foot trailers. The maximum payload capacity of most of them is 65 tons and the total combined weight of a wagon, trailers and cargo can run to 101 tons. The overhead clearance height of a loaded super flat can be over 17 feet.

The traditional method of loading/unloading trailers utilises a sloping ramp placed at the end of a stub track. Diesel tractors are used to push or pull the cumbersome trailers over the incline bridging the 42 inches between ground level and wagon deck. A string of coupled wagons is usually dealt with at one time, movable steel bridge plates affording an unbroken running surface from car to car. To secure trailers firmly in place on flat cars, special hitch assemblies are raised from the car deck to engage the trailer kingpins and chains are attached to the tandem axles.

The spectacular growth of piggyback has rendered the simple ramp method too slow. In the larger terminals it is replaced by huge power lifts on pneumatic tyres that move alongside the rake of wagons lifting the trailers on and off as required. One type straddles the wagons with steel legs and wheels on each side and works like an overhead crane; another type works from one side only. The cranes can load or unload 30-ton trailers at the rate of one every two minutes, permitting final reporting time only an hour in advance of train departure time.

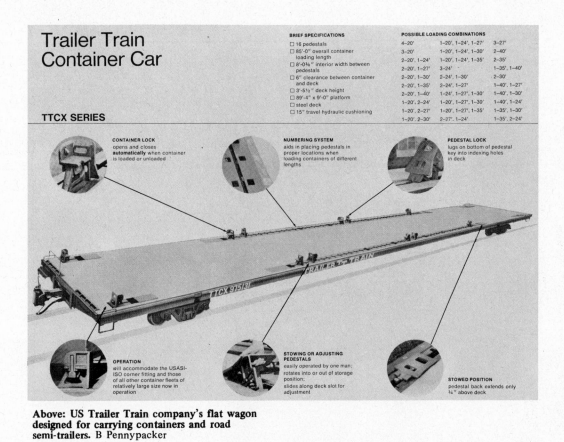

Trailer Train Container Car

TTCX SERIES

BRIEF SPECIFICATIONS
- □ 16 pedestals
- □ 85'-0" overall container loading length
- □ 8'-0⅜" interior width between pedestals
- □ 6" clearance between container and deck
- □ 3'-5½" deck height
- □ 89'-4" x 9'-0" platform
- □ steel deck
- □ 15" travel hydraulic cushioning

POSSIBLE LOADING COMBINATIONS

4–20'	1–20', 1–24', 1–27'	3–27'
3–20'	1–20', 1–24', 1–30'	2–40'
2–20', 1–24'	1–20', 1–24', 1–35'	2–35'
2–20', 1–27'	3–24'	1–35', 1–40'
2–20', 1–30'	2–24', 1–30'	2–30'
2–20', 1–35'	2–24', 1–27'	1–40', 1–27'
2–20', 1–40'	1–24', 1–27', 1–30'	1–40', 1–30'
1–20', 2–24'	1–20', 1–27', 1–30'	1–40', 1–24'
1–20', 2–27'	1–20', 1–27', 1–35'	1–35', 1–30'
1–20', 2–30'	2–27', 1–24'	1–35', 2–24'

CONTAINER LOCK
opens and closes **automatically** when container is loaded or unloaded

NUMBERING SYSTEM
aids in placing pedestals in proper locations when loading containers of different lengths

PEDESTAL LOCK
lugs on bottom of pedestal key into indexing holes in deck

TTCX 915131

TRAILER TRAIN

OPERATION
will accommodate the USASI-ISO corner fitting and those of all other container fleets of relatively large size now in operation

STOWING OR ADJUSTING PEDESTALS
easily operated by one man; rotates into or out of storage position; slides along deck slot for adjustment

STOWED POSITION
pedestal back extends only ¾" above deck

Above: US Trailer Train company's flat wagon designed for carrying containers and road semi-trailers. B Pennypacker

OL 40'0"
OH 13'6"
OW 8'0"
IL 39'6"
IH 8'10"
IW 7'8"
CU.FT. 2750
LT.WT. 11500

TRAILER TRAIN

The story of piggyback must necessarily include the story of Trailer Train Company, Chicago, which owns most of the wagons and leases them to all railroads, to move freely from time to time as needed and to Canada and Mexico. Pennsylvania Railroad and Norfolk & Western organised TT in 1956 and the Company is today owned by 33 railroads and one freight forwarding company. Representing a total investment of $900 million, is vast fleet of 60,000 cars includes COFC/TOFC flats, two- and three-level motorcar carriers which· have steel racks applied to the standard TOFC car, and other special types.

The largest part of the TT fleet is the TTX piggyback flat, of which there are 30,665. Designed principally to PRR specifications by Max Seel, Trailer Train's now-retired Manager of Engineering, today's TOFC flat costs nearly $18,000 and is built for TT by Pullman-Standard Company, Bethlehem Steel Company or ACF Industries. TTX cars are repaired and maintained at 23 contract shops located strategically on the various owner railroads. In 1970, the car fleet posted an amazing 97.8-per cent utilisation factor which was achieved with high maintenance standards, an average age of only seven years and high-demand service.

American railroads, in contrast to TT Company, have but 7,854 of their own piggyback cars, but they are also employed in through interline service to other railroads. Santa Fe and Southern Pacific/Cotton Belt are among the biggest fleet owners, with over 1,000 wagons each.

Across the border in Canada, TOFC is likewise a booming business, especially because great distances between cities, rugged terrain and severe winter weather make road haulage costly, time-consuming and downright hazardous. TOFC has given the trucker an inexpensive way out and one who might have hesitated to extend his routes westward across the Rockies can now do so with ease. But the Canadian approach to flat car equipment owned by railroads is conservative. The longest wagons are 63 feet, permitting the loading of one large trailer or two of the smaller 27-foot variety. It means more wagons or fewer trailers per train, but provides better flexibility in switching and routeing. Canadian National owns 1,060 flat cars and CP Rail (Canadian Pacific) has 1,600; they are not permitted off the home line.

With modest piggyback forms extant for many years, the fundamental reason for its sudden boom in the 1950s seems to be that the economic climate was ripe for such a technique. Rising wages and other operating costs, due largely to inflationary pressures, seemed almost automatically to send the big highway trailers scurrying to the TOFC ramps, where they could enjoy both lower ton-mile rates and faster delivery speed. The following figures compiled by the Association of American Railroads emphasise the phenomenal growth of the traffic:

Year	Wagonloads
1955	168,150
1960	554,115
1965	1,034,377
1971	1,196,519*

*Total number of trailers and containers handled 1,962,729.

Looking now at TOFC operations of several representative railroads, the pioneering Southern Pacific/Cotton Belt system is its inaugural piggybacking year of 1953 carried just 2,634 trailers and containers. By 1969 the total had soared to 270,079 units handled through 73 terminals — approximately half of all such traffic carried in the Western District of the United States. SP operates no all-TOFC trains but its busiest through routes, handling great quantities of flat-car trade in regular fast-scheduled service, run out of the largest terminal, Los Angeles, to San Francisco (470 miles), to Portland, Oregon (1,188 miles) and to St Louis, Missouri (2,446 miles). Blue Streak Merchandise is the train making the longest and fastest run — over the LA-St Louis route in 50½ hours, running via North Fort Worth, Texas and the Cotton Belt east of that point.

In the East, the Pennsylvania Railroad (now merged into Penn Central) was an early TOFC advocate with its fast-flying TrucTrains TT1/TT2 separating New York and Chicago by only 26 hours, which was but 10 hours more than it took the crack Broadway Limited to make the run. Serving the highly industrialised New England, Northeast and Middle West areas of America, Penn Central is the undisputed king of piggybacking, as its 34 terminals include the world's largest at Kearny, New Jersey, its daily fleet of 42 all-TOFC trains is by far the most on any road, and its total of 421,000 trailers and 80,000 Flexi-Van containers of mail represented more than 26 per cent of all piggyback business handled in America during 1971.

Now named TrailVan service, Penn Central's extensive operations employ a daily average of 2,700 Trailer Train wagons, plus its own Flexi-Van container flats for the long-distance bulk mail trains. While containers are universally transferable between ships, wheeled chassis and railway flat cars, the overwhelming emphasis in domestic service is to take the wheels along, for it has been found more convenient to use standard tandem-axle highway semi-trailers and therefore have the wheels right there at all times. Viewing TrailVan service with an optimistic nature, PC has recently invaded the short-haul market with a 6½-hour overnight run between Chicago and Detroit, Michigan, 272 miles.

By putting together PC's TrailVan train TV3 (New York to Rose Lake Yard in East St Louis, Illinois) and the Blue Streak Merchandise, we come up with a transcontinental running time of 79½ hours for the 3,496 miles between East and West coasts. But the 29-hour TV3 is not a through connection so additional time is required for the necessary transfer. PC traffic managers have found that Avon Yard in Indianapolis, Indiana, is the best gathering point for western connecting cars and trains MCB1/MCB1A run from that point right on through St Louis to the Cotton Belt and onward to Pine Bluff, Arkansas, 401 miles deep in Cotton Belt territory. Even the locomotives go through and in this respect, PC engines have occasionally been seen as far away as Los Angeles. Conversely, SP and CB engines often get as far east as Harrisburg, Pennsylvania, 856 miles from their home rails.

Right: A Southern Pacific piggyback train with the Rockies in the background.
Southern Pacific RR

Below: Piggyback CN style.

Overall speed in long-distance TOFC service relies on elimination of the delays of interchanging wagons from one railroad to another. Such a service is exemplified by the Transcontinental Highball, a unique run-through collaboration of three railroads to forward piggyback and other priority freight between the Richmond, Virginia, area and California points. The train leaves Richmond each morning at 08.30 via Seaboard Coast Line; the second day finds it at Memphis, Tennessee, on the Frisco Lines; by a minute before midnight of the fourth day, it has arrived in Los Angeles as Santa Fe train 668.

Norfolk & Western's share of piggyback traffic in 1971 came to 186,778 trailers loaded at 52 on-line ramps. While this predominantly Midwestern railroad reaches the Eastern seaboard only in the Norfolk, Virginia, area, by means of advantageous connections with other roads, N&W can compete effectively with Baltimore & Ohio and Penn Central which serve directly the manufacturing and seaport centres of New York, Philadelphia and Baltimore.

Looking at the Canadian traffic scene, total TOFC wagonloadings for 1971, not including containers, were 185,560 in a service that is growing at the rate of about ten per cent a year, although it is quite modest in volume compared to American figures. CP Rail can get a

piggyback flat car across Canada from Saint John or Frederickton, (New Brunswick) to Vancouver, (British Columbia) in 5½ days. The longest possible run is 3,754 rail miles via Canadian National from Halifax (Nova Scotia) to Vancouver, but such a haul, of containers from ships, would probably be a so-called 'land bridge' operation to another ship at Vancouver, thus avoiding the time of an all-water journey through the Panama Canal. Fast overnight service is run between major cities of the busy Eastern manufacturing provinces of Ontario and Quebec, with the largest piggyback terminals located in Montreal.

Canadian National has handled American TOFC traffic to Whittier (Alaska) and the Alaska Railroad, via Prince Rupert (British Columbia) and CNR's Aquatrain ships. In September 1971, CNR opened a new ship-to-rail container terminal at Halifax, thereby offering faster and cheaper general freight service to inland cities than could be offered if the ships continued onward via the St Lawrence Seaway, which since its opening in 1959 has been strangling the life out of Halifax as a seaport. But the strange paradox of it all is that this relatively new CNR COFC service is an example of the government competing against itself, for both railway and seaway have been built, owned and operated at the cost of hundreds of millions of dollars of public funds.

Amtrak
US NATIONALISED RAIL SERVICE

At midnight on April 30, 1971, an Act of Congress setting up a nationalised rail passenger corporation came into force in the United States of America. Instantly, more than two-thirds of all passenger trains running in the United States ceased to exist, and the majority of the survivors, amounting to a mere 184 long-distance trains, passed into semi-public ownership.

Famous names, like the City of Los Angeles, San Francisco Chief, Hawkeye, Capitol Limited, Pocahontas, and Pennsylvania Limited, disappeared overnight and are unlikely to reappear in the future. The former American network of passenger trains, at its peak in the 1936-41 period when it totalled 15,000 each day, had eroded to barely 500 trains early in 1971, and then, at one fell swoop, dwindled to the 184 figure which the new administration accepted, fortunately as rock bottom.

When quasi-nationalisation was mooted, the title 'Railpax' was intended for the corporation, but it was later changed to AMTRAK (American trackage) once the Act was passed. The new body took over the long-distance passenger trains of those companies opting to join, but no compulsion was exercised, so that a few remained in private hands, including the Southern Railway, the Rock Island, and the Denver & Rio Grande. Most intense operator of passenger trains in the United States, mainly over short hauls but up to 117 miles, the Long Island Rail Road, already belonged to the State of New York and — operated by Metropolitan Transit — remained outside AMTRAK.

Before AMTRAK was formed, virtually all railroads claimed that their passenger trains were losing money fast, but that freight services paid. They had, in fact, been loading all possible costs against passenger operations on an accountancy basis not unknown in Britain.

Opposite Page: One method of loading/unloading piggyback trains in the FWD-Wagner Piggy Packer, here seen at work for SP at Los Angeles. Southern Pacific Railroad.

Below: New York-Washington Metroliner in AMTRAK colours. K Westcott-Jones.

Amtrak Routes at the start (May 1971)

◯	Designated end point cities
▫	Route identification points
− − − −	Added Amtrak service
• • • • •	Experimental Amtrak Route
⬤⬤⬤⬤⬤	Non-Amtrak railroads

Amtrak ➤

America's first nationwide passenger rail system

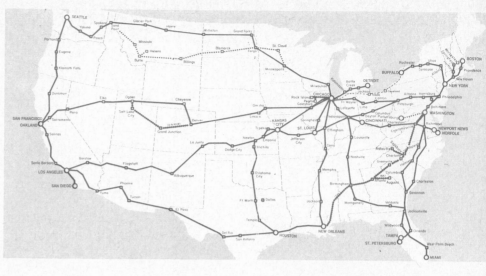

Above: The new logo for AMTRAK used on rolling stock and as direction signs at stations. J R Batts

Right: Denver Zephyr of the Burlington Northern (Chicago, Burlington & Quincy) at Denver in July 1970. V Goldberg

Below: Another pre-AMTRAK train, the Burlington Northern (Northern Pacific) North Coast Limited, at Livingstone in July 1970. V Goldberg

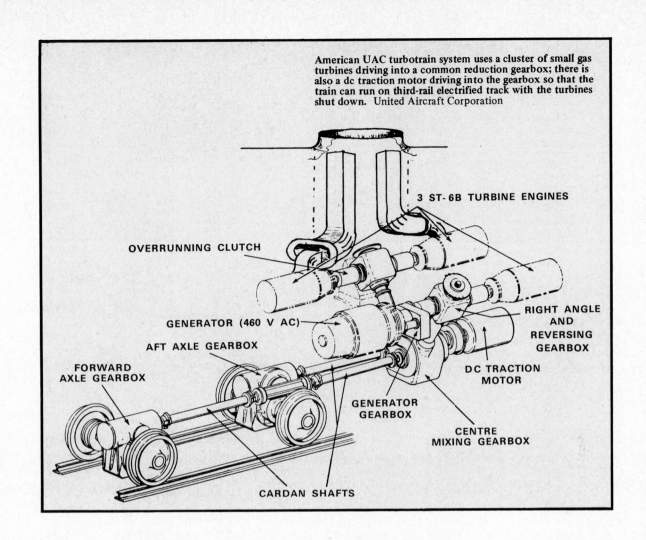

American UAC turbotrain system uses a cluster of small gas turbines driving into a common reduction gearbox; there is also a dc traction motor driving into the gearbox so that the train can run on third-rail electrified track with the turbines shut down. United Aircraft Corporation

3 ST-6B TURBINE ENGINES

OVERRUNNING CLUTCH

GENERATOR (460 V AC)

AFT AXLE GEARBOX

FORWARD AXLE GEARBOX

RIGHT ANGLE AND REVERSING GEARBOX

DC TRACTION MOTOR

GENERATOR GEARBOX

CENTRE MIXING GEARBOX

CARDAN SHAFTS

UAC three-car turbotrain for trial running on American tracks for the US Department of Transportation. United Aircraft Corporation

But six companies, known to many railway men and enthusiastic passengers as 'the half-dozen good guys', had maintained efficient and comfortable passenger trains to the last. They were the Santa Fe, Burlington Northern, Union Pacific, Seaboard Atlantic, Baltimore & Ohio–Chesapeake & Ohio, and Southern. The first five became AMTRAK members, their crack trains handed over, while the Southern, stayed out. But those opting out had to promise that their standards would be maintained at least until 1975, with frequencies and service not less than those applying in 1971. With the Southern there are no worries, for it is a profitable company and runs its crack train ('Candy Varnish' in American railroad parlance), the Southern Crescent, as a worthy operation.

Not unnaturally, the first AMTRAK trains were formed from the best rolling stock of joining companies, but others, of course, provided their equipment. AMTRAK decided to buy the best 1,200 cars from member companies, to refurbish them, and to paint them in the agreed new colours of red, white, and blue with the arrow-type AMTRAK logo. The organisation also decided to order 78 new motive power units, for delivery in 1973/74. At first, however, rail customers noticed little difference except for long gaps in the timetables. Those trains still surviving tended to be cosmopolitan mixtures of different companies' rolling stock, much shorter than before, and usually with head-end revenue vehicles missing (because mail and railway express business does not come under AMTRAK).

The first timetable, AMTRAK One, was a disappointment to many, and not easy to read. But it must be emphasised that it was rock-bottom, the end of the decline, and what was to follow would at least move upwards. It did, very slightly. AMTRAK took a long time to get under way, and almost immediately encountered stiff opposition and resistance from traditional railmen. The old companies continued to haul the trains and to provide crews, some of whom clearly did not understand and did not bother to learn what the new regime was all about.

Former airline executives were recruited to senior positions in the AMTRAK organisation, which was based in Washington's L'Enfant Plaza under the wing of the nearby US Department of Transportation. It was a direct reversal of the process of the 1950s when airlines lured away top railroad men and so weakened the rail companies on the passenger side that they lost their dynamic quality. Marketing was the main aim in the early days of AMTRAK, with passenger advertising appearing for the first time in years ('We're making the trains fun to ride again' was the best known) and travel agency commission paid on ticket sales above fifteen dollars.

It was not until the winter timetables of 1971-72 that AMTRAK could be seen to be moving forward. Over 200 trains were shown, and the highlights were all on the Boston to Miami lines, with great emphasis on the Metroliners running to Washington and the long-distance trains to Florida. The de luxe Florida Special, upgraded in all respects, had its best season for many years. The Broadway Limited between New York and Chicago over the Penn-Central line was improved and began to recapture custom, while some progress was made with various states to subsidise a train service beyond Buffalo to

Cleveland (the largest American city left without passenger trains after AMTRAK began) and Chicago.

AMTRAK 4, the timetable for the early months of 1972, showed 215 trains (although the Cleveland service disappeared again) and the restoration of that famous overnight Mid American streamliner, the Panama Limited, over the metals of the Illinois Central from Chicago to New Orleans. The New York-Washington Metroliners became the highlights of AMTRAK, clearly profitable and successful, and now increased to 14 services each way daily. Standardisation was gaining favour and one scoring point for the new administration was getting all long-distance passenger trains into and out of Chicago to use one station (Union) instead of six, as previously. Only commuter services still operate into the Illinois Central station, while Rock Island's commuter and medium-distance trains (which are non-AMTRAK) continue to be the only users of forlorn La Salle Street.

Meal prices were fixed as far as possible, also those for drinks, soft and hard, and hot snacks in the snack-bar cars. About 50 young women, dressed in smart uniforms with the red, white and blue AMTRAK insignia, rode various trains as passenger service representatives, a sort of super-stewardess, to help people with problems, smooth out journeys, and act as liaison between train crews and the quasi-government organisation. Taking a leaf from the airlines book, the AMTRAK girls wore hot pants on the Florida trains, and thick jackets and blue trousers on the northern routes.

There is still widespread criticism of AMTRAK and the Act which created it, the main charge by Americans being that the Act was so written as to enable railroads to give up most of their passenger trains instead of improving rail service to the public. But regular users of the surviving trains have noted a definite improvement in service and most report the feeling that, now, someone cares. However, AMTRAK and its enthusiastic officials have not yet established sufficient authority over die-hard railroad men of the old companies and spend a great deal of time battling to get things done in new ways. Their enthusiasm, based on former airline experience, sometimes leads to unfortunate situations, when, for example, a good train formation is ordered, but old hands stubbornly fit the dome cars facing the wrong way, or fail to tell the newcomers that chosen cars from varying companies might not match up when being coupled.

Financing of AMTRAK, which is really a Government corporation, was by Federal moneys plus sums deposited by the member railway companies. Some say the joining companies gladly paid up to be rid of their passenger trains and there could be some truth in that. A weakness of AMTRAK is that, so far, no one has forced the companies to make good the damage to track caused by their excessively long freight trains. By overloading and overworking lines, without much maintenance, freight has been made to pay big profits, but some tracks are so bad they cannot be used by passenger trains. Even once-famous main lines on which steam expresses thundered at 80 miles an hour in the early 1950s are restricted to 30 miles an hour for passenger workings.

The AMTRAK summer timetable of 1972 gave definite indications of advance, with the former Santa Fe's Super Chief de luxe streamliner running as a separate unit, followed by the all-coach (second-class) El Capitan in high-level cars, and then the Chief, a mixed Pullman/coach consist. Over the same line to Kansas City each summer day rolled the Texas Chief, also Pullman coach. It began to look a bit like old times, with the pleasing fact that good passenger loads were carried and satisfied customers began writing to AMTRAK authorities.

Going cap-in-hand to the Senate Appropriations Committee in the spring of 1972, AMTRAK got nearly twice as much money as it asked for, an almost unique event in US Government circles. But it is, charged, as a corporation, with turning in a profit by 1975, and at present the losses are very heavy. People are not yet returning to the trains in great enough numbers, although there is a percentage gain. No attack on airlines, except with the high-speed Metroliners, is intended. Both airline and railway authorities point out that if a mere two per cent of road users taking their own cars were persuaded into planes and trains equally, all airline losses would cease and AMTRAK would double its services.

Canada has been cut off completely from any rail links with the United States since AMTRAK took over, but moves are afoot to restore the Seattle-Vancouver International trains and a service to Montreal from Albany. In the Niagara area, a once-daily Toronto, Hamilton and Buffalo train has been running again but Niagara Falls station is closed and the tracks torn up.

Supporters of AMTRAK believe the year 1973 will see the big breakthrough to success, but it has first to convince Americans that riding trains is worthwhile again. So many years of neglect by railroad companies, plus aggressive advertising by airlines and the demands of the automotive industry (on which so much of America's economy is based and which accounts for 22 per cent of employment), have turned a tremendous number of Americans away from the rails. They have to be won back by good service, punctual arrivals, and reasonable frequencies. AMTRAK believe the climate is right, with anti-pollution voices raised everywhere in the land against the continued use of private cars, and the worries about flying caused by literally hundreds of hi-jackings and delays forced by security checks, apart from overcrowded airways in the vicinity of the busiest airports.

Foreign visitors are among the heaviest users of American trains. Recently a head count on the Coastal Daylight, a dome-car AMTRAK train from Los Angeles to San Francisco, showed 103 passengers, all but four of them non-Americans. But it has to be made easier to buy AMTRAK tickets at travel agencies abroad, while frequencies need improving on long hauls, as well as timings. All too many passenger trains start their journeys at unattractive early morning hours, or arrive very late at night; one of the worst offenders is the non-AMTRAK Rio Grande with its thrice-weekly train from Denver to Salt Lake City through the most magnificent scenery in the United States.

Top opposite page: Smartly uniformed stewardess serving in the club car of AMTRAK's Metroliner. K Westcott-Jones.

Below: Rear end of Southern Pacific diesel streamliner at San Francisco in 1952. J M Jarvis.

RAILWAYS OF CANADA

Canadian National Railways or CN, as it is known colloquially, is an amalgamation of many predecessor companies. In contrast with Canadian Pacific, it was not conceived as a nationwide system, although some of its principal components eventually grew to meet that description. The formation of CNR took place in stages in the period 1918-1923. The new system included three major components (and several minor constituents), namely, the Canadian Northern Railway (CNoR), a Canadian enterprise; the Canadian Government Railways (CGR), in public ownership; and Grand Trunk Railway (GTR), an English-owned system.

The Grand Trunk was the oldest established of the three, and included Canada's first railway, the Champlain & St Lawrence, a portage railway linking the St Lawrence river, opposite Montreal, with the Lake Champlain river system at St Johns. Built to a gauge of 5ft 6in, it opened on July 21, 1836, with an English locomotive, *Dorchester*, four American coaches and Montreal-built wagons. For several decades, the 5ft 6in gauge was widely used in Canada, and it was adopted by the Grand Trunk when it opened in 1856. The GTR was conceived as a main line linking Upper and Lower Canada (Ontario and Quebec), and was built to high standards. Extensions to its main line between Toronto and Montreal, and the take-over of other companies

eventually brought it west to Chicago in the USA, and east to Quebec and beyond. All its track was converted to standard gauge by 1874. However, the railway was far from being an unqualified success financially, despite its 4,800 route-miles.

Two late-Victorian Canadian entrepreneurs, William MacKenzie and Donald Mann, fathered the Canadian Northern Railway. From a small group of lines in Manitoba, the CNoR expanded, in less than two decades, to an 8,000-mile transcontinental system, most of it new construction, but incorporating some existing local lines. Booming immigration spurred the growth, but it was supported also by public and government desires that transcontinental traffic should not be wholly dependent on the Canadian Pacific.

Canada is unique in the railway field in possessing, side by side, two major railway systems, one publicly owned, the other in private hands. Early examples of public ownership (and, indeed, construction) were found in the maritime colonies of Nova Scotia and New Brunswick. A rail link with Canada East and West (ie Lower and Upper Canada) was a requirement for the inclusion of those colonies in the Dominion of Canada, just as British Columbia needed the construction of the Canadian Pacific.

The Intercolonial Railway (ICR as the eastern link became) was finally completed in 1875 as a standard-gauge line, although certain of its components had earlier been built to the 5ft 6in gauge. Its route lay close to the shore of the St Lawrence, well away from the US border. The ICR was a sizeable unit of the Canadian Government Railways, but the National Trans-continental Railway (NTR) was longer. Its route — deliberately circuitous to open up formerly untapped areas — ran through Northern Ontario and Quebec, linking Winnipeg with Quebec City, and on east to Moncton, New Brunswick.

A subsidiary of the Grand Trunk, the Grand Trunk Pacific (GTP) was built west from Winnipeg, to reach the Pacific at the new port of Prince Rupert, through country much of which was ready for immediate development. The completion in 1915 of this new trans-continental route (which was built from the start to mainline standards) followed the outbreak of the 1914-18 war. In consequence, the tide of immigrants upon which the newly-opened railways depended, ceased, with dire consequences for much of Canada's railway network. The war-time traffic boom came only in already developed areas; Halifax, Nova Scotia, for example, became a vital port in the route to Europe.

The new lines, the CNoR, the NTR, and the GTP, quickly experienced financial problems, such that the CNoR passed to the control of the CGR late in 1918. The combined system started to be called Canadian National Railways early in 1919, and the GTP, after being placed in receivership in that year, came under CNR management in 1920. Management of the GTR itself passed in 1922 to the CNR and late the same year the name Canadian National Railways was formally adopted. In January 1923, all the constituents were legally amalgamated.

Most of the CNR components had included smaller secondary railways taken over in a variety of circumstances over the years. Space permits mention only of two of particular interest. Railways in the then colony of Prince Edward Island were sponsored by the island's government, and a 3ft 6in-gauge system developed there from 1874 had reached a mileage of 278 by 1912. In an island only 120 miles long, and never more than 25 miles wide, financial problems were in evidence from the start, and a condition of the entry of Prince Edward Island to the dominion in 1873 was that the dominion assumed responsibility for the PEI Railway. It was placed in ICR hands, so eventually becoming part of the CN system. Conversion to standard gauge was spread over the period 1919-1930. Today, train ferries link the island with the mainland, and although, alas, passenger services have recently ceased, the aura of the narrow gauge lingers on in the island.

Left: One of the five Canadian-built seven-car UAC turbo-trains used on Montreal-Toronto services for short periods in 1968-69 and 1970-71. B Jackson

Below: A modern ML-Worthington diesel-electric loco-motive of Canadian Pacific heads a passenger train out of Montreal. D T Rowe

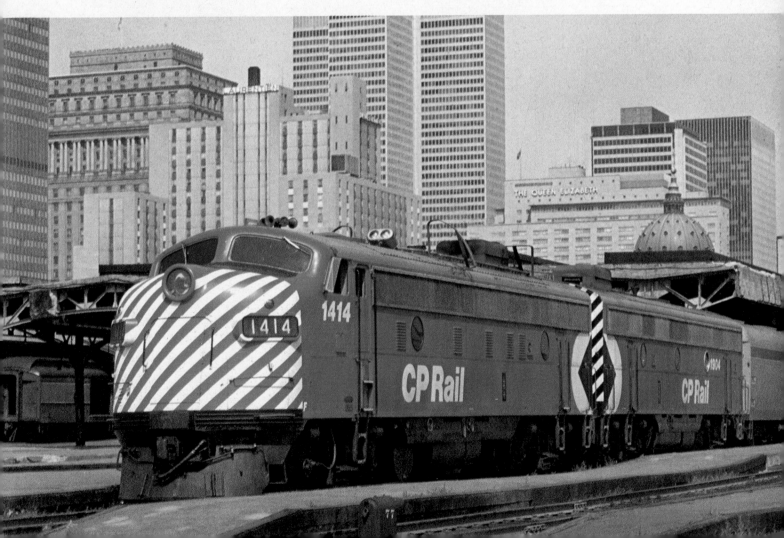

Newfoundland is an island the size of England. It claims to be Britain's oldest colony and Canada's newest province. The railway came late to "Newfie" — 1884, but eventually over 900 miles of 3ft 6in-gauge track crossed the island, and branched out to some of the coastal communities. Of narrow gauge to this day, the system, after a chequered career, first in private hands and then under the Newfoundland government, passed to CN when Newfoundland joined the confederation in 1949. Although mileage has shrunk to 700 and passenger service is confined now to mixed trains. Train ferries provide a link with the island's increasing freight traffic, and freight can be transhipped at Port aux Basques, the island ferry terminal, or trucks (bogies) can be changed on dual-gauge sidings.

A few other lines of local interest also passed to CN Hands after 1923, but we must now look at CN's major traffic centres. Focal points of the system are Moncton (for the Maritime provinces), Montreal and Toronto (for Quebec and Ontario respectively) and Winnipeg, for the Prairie provinces. Major freight marshalling yards are located at these four points — with many other yards elsewhere.

In the passenger field, CN has had the best-filled timetable folder in N America for many years. With a system route-mileage now of 25,000, and many hundreds of miles of new lines built since the war, this is, perhaps, not surprising. In addition to transcontinental service linking Montreal and Toronto with Vancouver, CN serves the "trunk" corridor Quebec-Montreal-Toronto-SW Ontario, where much of Canada's population, industry and agriculture are located.

System headquarters is in Montreal, where the modern Central station offers appropriate facilities for the traveller. There, also, is the only electrified part of the system, an 18-mile suburban line, with a 3-mile-long tunnel under Mount Royal, equipped with a 2,400V dc overhead system.

Toronto has some surburban rail service along the lake shore, provided by CN Over its tracks under contract to the Government of Ontario, with the title GO Transit. On its own account, CN operates just a handful of local trains around Toronto. Other areas of passenger activity include the Maritimes, served by the well-known Ocean Limited and the Scotian trains, and northern areas where highways are lacking.

Rolling stock on Canadian National Railways has followed North American practice for many years, although a number of English features were in evidence in early days. With so many different constituents, the steam locomotive fleet was quite varied. At its peak it numbered 3,260 locomotives, but the figure later settled down to about 2,500. Perhaps best known were upwards of 200 4-8-4s, half of which dated from the 1940s, and most of which survived to the end of steam in 1960. In order of totals, 2-8-0s (850), 2-8-2s (500), 4-6-0s (600) and Pacifics (330) filled out the fleet, with other types less in evidence. A particularly Canadian feature in more recent construction was the fully enclosed cab to provide protection against the Northern winter. Dieselisation took place late (compared with the US) and quickly, in the period 1951-1960.

Passenger stock also followed conventional N American practice. A change from an all-over dark green livery to an attractive green-gold-black livery coincided with an extensive order for over 350 modern streamlined passenger coaches in the mid-1950s. A few years later, a modern corporate image was adopted, with a new CN device and passenger coaches finished in black and white, with bright reds and blues internally.

A large fleet (105,000) of freight wagons, all of bogie type, rounds off CN's rolling stock. The fleet includes many with carrying capacity up to 100 tons, and specialised types to deal with particular traffics. Diesel locomotives number over 2,000 and are of standard North American builders' designs, although incorporating some internal modifications to cater for the extremes of Canadian weather.

CN's activities are not confined to rails. Again, like British Railways, there is a railway-owned hotel chain in principal cities, and coastal shipping activities are extensive, particularly in the east. Newfoundland's coast is well served, and several ferry services are operated elsewhere on the Atlantic seaboard. The SS *"Prince George"* provides a link to Alaska on the Pacific, as well as barge service to link up with CN's isolated freight lines on Vancouver Island. CN is also active in the telecommunications field, and until recently, "fathered" the national airline Air Canada.

In its earlier days, CN had a conservative reputation, but it was an instrument of government social policy. Today, the federal regulatory body, the Canadian Transportation Commission, is studying the role of each mode in the field of transport. One can rest assured that this well-run railway, today a leader in the North American railway field, will continue to be a vital part of Canada's economy. Its courageous stand in the 1960s in respect of passenger service, and its (qualified) intentions to continue to serve the passenger market, is an object lesson which might well be noted elsewhere.

The activities of the CPR now extend far beyond the original concept, for the company operates international air and shipping services, has vast mining and property interests and provides telecommunications, road haulage and hotel services, in addition to its railways. Even so, CP railways today extend to over 21,000 miles of route. The title CP Rail and a new CP device have been adopted for most of the company's rail activities in Canada.

From its headquarters at Windsor station in Montreal, a main line extending through Toronto to Windsor (for Detroit) is now a freight-only route competing with CNR. Until the last decade, Toronto-Montreal/Ottawa passenger train services of CNR and CPR were co-ordinated and operated in pool. Also, in Canada's main corridor, CPR extends to Quebec City, again in competition with CNR, but there passenger trains still run, three times daily, to Quebec's ornate Palais station. From Montreal also there is passenger service along the North Shore (of the Ottawa River) to Ottawa, in addition to that via Vankleek Hill on the transcontinental route. There is also suburban service on the Vanleek Hill route as far as Vaudrevil (40 miles from Montreal). Base service is operated by diesel railcars helped out in the peaks by conventional hauled stock, and by a handful of double-deck coaches worked push-pull.

East from Montreal there is overnight service to and from Saint John, NB, by the Atlantic Limited and a CP

Top: A Canadian National vintage 'combination' car for mixed-train service at Charlottetown, Prince Edward Island in May 1968. V Goldberg   Above: Stephenson-built 5ft 6in-gauge 'Prospero' for (Canadian) Great Western in 1866, later passed to (Canadian) Midland Railway. 'NG' is to warn shunters of the presence in the train of narrow-gauge (4ft 8½in) stock. Canadian National Railways (P Wood)

route which is about 260 miles shorter than CN's route via the ex-Intercolonial line along the Gulf of St Lawrence. At Saint John, service continues to Digby, NS (48 miles), across the Bay of Fundy with its 40ft tides, by the MV *Princess of Acadia.* (This vessel and the Pacific Coast coastal streamers are operated by CP Rail and no CP Steamships.)

At Digby Wharf connection is made with the CP-owned, but separate (both physically and operationally) Dominion Atlantic Railway, which extends 217 miles from Yarmouth to Halifax. The branch line from Windsor to Truro sees one of the very few surviving mixed passenger and freight trains in North America. The mainline DAR passenger service is operated by two intensively worked diesel mu trains, lettered Dominion Atlantic Railway.

Another independently operated member of the CP Rail family in the east is the Quebec Central Railway, which links Quebec City with Sherbrooke (148 miles) on the Montreal-Saint John line. The QCR serves the vast asbestos mines which provide it with much of its traffic.

In SW Ontario, two further members of the CP family are the Grand River Railway and the Lake Erie & Northern Railway, which both run out of the city of Galt, respectively north to Waterloo (14 miles) and south to Brantford (21 miles). The former frequent electric inter-urban (express tramcar) passenger services are long gone and the remaining freight trains have been dieselised for a decade. In the same area is the branch to Owen Sound (129 miles), once the narrow-gauge (3ft 6in) Toronto, Grey & Bruce Railway. it became part of CPR in 1884. Traces of the old narrow-gauge formation can still be found, where they were discarded after conversion to standard gauge at the end of 1881.

Farther west, beyond the grain-shipping lake-head ports at Thunder Bay, CP Rail operates a complex network of branch lines in the Prairie provinces. Some of them now see little more than seasonal use after the grain harvest. Branch-line passenger services there are now confined to twice-daily trips between Calgary and Edmonton (194 miles). From Edmonton, the Northern Alberta Railways stretch farther north over several

Above: CPR Pacific No 2468 at Toronto roundhouse in 1952. J M Jarvis

numerous workaday 2-8-2s and 2-8-0s provided the backbone for freight service. For secondary lines, a large fleet of 4-6-0s, of Class D10 and others powered trains across the system. Much of the passenger equipment was of conventional heavyweight construction but forward-looking smooth-sided coaches were introduced in the 1930s; regrettably, much of the fine coach fleet has recently been sold although the 173 stainless-steel cars purchased in 1954-5 cover most of the surviving loco-hauled services. There is also a fleet of 54 diesel railcars and over 1,100 diesel locomotives.

Freight stock totals about 80,000 wagons of conventional North American design, with a high proportion of specialised and high-capacity types. Forest products, grain, coal, ores and manufactured goods all provide traffic for CP Rail's nationwide system, on which freight provides about 90 per cent of the revenue.

Below: CN narrow-gauge (3ft 6in) coaches at Bishop's Falls, Newfoundland, in September 1967. V Goldberg

Bottom: CN Diesel-electric locomotive No 6528 pictured near Montreal. J R Batts

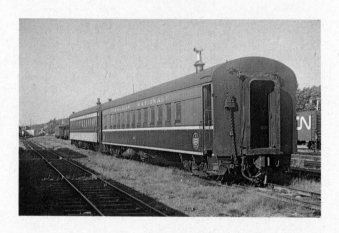

routes, totalling 923 miles, into an area with much mineral and agricultural promise. The NAR is owned jointly by CP Rail and CNR.

In the South of Alberta, west from Medicine Hat and over Crow's Nest pass, extends the Kettle Valley route of CP Rail. It crosses the Rocky Mountains close to the US border. Since its completion at the turn of the century, it has provided an alternative to the original transcontinental route, which it rejoins at Spence's Bridge. Freight only now, it serves the fruit-growing and mining areas in southern British Columbia. In the heart of this mountainous area, there still survives an isolated railway to Nakusp, linked to the rest of the system by car floats on Slocan lake.

In 1971, CP Rail was seriously considering electrification of its main line through the Rockies west of Calgary. Coal, bound for Japan from British Columbia mines is the reason behind the proposal: a supplementary new port, Roberts Bank, new Vancouver, is already under construction.

Vancouver is the terminus of the transcontinental route, and is home base to the Pacific Coastal steamer services, now much reduced in extent. However, year-round ferry service links Vancouver with Nanaimo, on Vancouver Island. Nanaimo is situated at about mid-point on CP Rail's most westerly outpost, the Esquimalt & Nanaimo Railway, which links Victoria with Courtenay (140 miles); a single diesel railcar provides daily passenger service.

The foregoing has summarised CP's railway activities over 16,000 miles of route in Canada, but brief mention should be made of CP's 57 per cent interest in the 4,700-mile SOO Line Railroad, a US-based company which covers an area between Chicago and Winnipeg, and east to Sault Ste Marie, between Lake Superior and Lake Huron.

In the matter of equipment, CP was unusual in North America in building its own steam locomotives and passenger coaches. Its Delorimier and, later, the Angus shops, both in Montreal, built quality products of traditional designs. Of the steam locomotive fleet (which numbered 1,962 in 1937) the large Selkirks (2-10-4s) and Royal Hudsons (4-6-4s) are well recorded, but

ESQUIMALT & NANAIMO RAILWAY

Originally intended (in 1875) as part of the transcontinental route, the Esquimalt and Nanaimo Railway was part of the inducement to British Columbia to join the Canadian confederation. Incorporation eventually took place in 1884 and by 1886 the line was open between Victoria and Wellington, where there were coal mines. Wellington is five miles north of Nanaimo, second largest community on Vancouver Island. Esquimalt is a naval base near Victoria.

Canadian Pacific acquired the E&N in 1905. Its independent founders had included Californians Colis P Huntington and Leland Stanford, both closely associated with the Central Pacific line, which formed the western end of the first transcontinental railway in the United States. With the E&N there came to CP a substantial provincial land grant, of 1.4 million acres.

By Edwardian times, the forestry industries on the island were booming, and Canadian Pacific extended the E&N, firstly in 1910, along the coast to Parksville (18 miles). The line was extended a further 40 miles across the island, in 1911, to Port Alberni, a westcoast port situated at the head of the Alberni inlet. The approach to the port by rail is steeply graded and circuitous as the track descends from the watershed.

In 1912, a branch line from Hayward, just north of Duncan, was built 18 miles west to Lake Cowichan. Finally, in 1914 a further 45-mile extension was built up the East Coast from Parksville to Courtenay, present northern terminal of the E&N, leaving Port Alberni on a branch line. Route mileage with spurs now totals just 200.

The island location of the E&N of course isolates it from other CP Rail lines, but a short spur south of Nanaimo takes the tracks down to a ferry ship, where train and car ferries maintain connections to the mainland at Vancouver.

Passenger services on the E&N since the mid-nineteen-fifties, have been worked by RDC and are now confined to the main Victoria-Courtenay run (140 miles), much of which closely follows the east coast of the island. One round trip daily is worked, Monday to Saturdays. The journey is scenic, and the line climbs to over 900ft, at Malahat, only 20 miles out of Victoria (at sea level) before following a more gentle route along the coast.

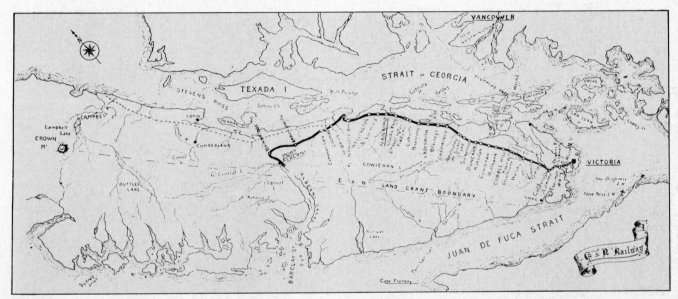

A CP Rail Budd stainless-steel RDC similar to those now operated on Esquimalt & Nanaimo line. L S Williams

103

Above, left and below: Three pictures of logging operations in the Nanaimo river area of Vancouver Island, British Columbia. All Jennings Ltd

CANADIAN NATIONAL
Super Continental

Unlike Europe, where the recent trend has been towards consolidation, and even expansion, of high-quality inter-city rail services, in North America the long-distance passenger train has been allowed to decline almost to extinction. The fabled Limiteds, Zephyrs, Hiawatha and so on, many of which not only lasted into, but reached peaks of performance, in the diesel age, are gone or are but pale and shabby shadows of their former glory.

Now government-backed efforts are being made to bring about a revival. Initially the impetus was the serious slowing down of travel on the busiest inter-city routes caused by gross overcrowding of roads and air-ports; more recently the support for a programme of passenger railway rejuvenation has had the broader aim of avoiding or reducing the huge costs, both financial and environmental, of meeting all travel needs by road and air services only. Hence, in the United States of America, where free enterprise is enshrined, what amounts to a nationalised inter-city passenger train network was recently established.

Across the border in Canada events have been generally similar, but with more determined efforts to retain efficient passenger railways the decline has not been so complete. In fact Canada continues to operate the only two remaining truly trans-continental expresses in North America. One of them is the subject of our picture on the following pages, the Super Continental of Canadian National Railways; the other is the rival Canadian Pacific Railway's train the Canadian.

The Super Continental operates daily throughout the year between Montreal and Toronto in the east and Vancouver in the west, taking a route via Winnipeg, Edmonton and the Jasper National Park in the Rocky Mountains. The train is scheduled to cover the 2,914 miles from Montreal to Vancouver in a shade over 72 hours; the through portion from Toronto, which joins the main train at Capreol, takes about two hours less.

Passenger amenities provided on the train include children's playroom, club car, sleeping coaches and restaurant and cafeteria services and, on the Edmonton -Jasper-Vancouver section, double-deck dome observation coaches. In consist, the Super Continental dwarfs most European passenger trains, loading up to a gross 1,400 tons with up to 20 or so coaches and two- or three-unit locomotive power.

Only a very few miles of main-line railway in North America are electrified and Canadian National's express passenger services are exclusively diesel hauled. The Super Continental in the picture is multiple headed by Canadian-built Type 6500 3,500hp diesel-electric locomotives which entered service in 1956. The photograph shows the train threading a gorge in the Rockies, near Jasper, Alberta, with Mount Robson, at 12,972ft the highest peak of the Canadian Rockies, in the background.

Lounge or club cars have been a feature of CN rail travel for many years. Here is a picture of one introduced in 1947, Canadian National Railways

A train threading a gorge in the Canadian Rockies near Jasper Alberta. Canadian National Railways.

THE PACIFIC GREAT EASTERN

The Pacific Great Eastern Railway, which runs 978 miles from Vancouver nearly to the Yukon border in British Columbia, flees from the shore of the Pacific after only 50 miles, is rather less than 'Great', and is not, obviously, 'Eastern'. But it is certainly a railway.

It is unsurprising that the PGE, like all well-loved and easily forgiven institutions, should have had its initials irreverently interpreted by the public to mean 'Please Go Easy', 'Past God's Endurance', and 'Prince George Eventually' — the city of Prince George having been for years its projected terminal, 466 miles from Vancouver and exactly in the centre of the enormous Western province of Canada, 359,000 square miles in area but populated today by only 2.2 million souls.

The odd name for the odd railway, mostly single-line and reaching a speed of 50 miles an hour only over about 100 miles, comes from the Great Eastern Railway in Britain. The motive for the christening can be regarded as similar to that of the parent who named his son after an affluent and elderly uncle. 'The somewhat obscure connection with the Great Eastern', says PGE general manager Joe S Broadbent, 'can be gleaned from a press report dated January 30, 1914, which recorded that the PGE debenture of $7,250,000 had been heavily subscribed in London.'

With that kind of money at stake, many orphans have been saddled with worse names.

The PGE is now a prosperous diesel-powered carrier of freight, but of very few passengers, with a net profit in 1971 of nearly $1 million, and Broadbent says the initials should stand for 'Progressively Greater Earnings' — in an era when railways are feeling the pinch.

But before modernisation, the affection for a wayward and fuddling 'character' was enjoyed by the PGE, and nobody can say it was undeserved. Railway buffs, in fact, elected the PGE to world-wide renown, and there were countless visits, up to 1950, by clubs of railway lovers to savour what they knew was the 'end of an era', to be enjoyed only on that funny railway in British Columbia.

What did the PGE offer that was so attractively olde-world? Well, it was still possible, before modernisation, to sit in a coach heated by a wood-burning stove and lit by swinging oil lamps. Indeed, there were times when the passengers, eager for exercise, jumped from the train at fuelling stops and helped the train crew load up with logs cut from the surrounding forests by the obliging, and well-paid, local Indians.

In summer, the PGE boasted an 'observation car'. To the delight of sophisticated passengers from the great Limiteds of the USA, it proved to be a flat freight wagon equipped with wooden benches, somewhat like the top deck of the old open tramcar, unspoiled by any shelter overhead or at the sides. In the 100-degree heat of high summer, there was nothing more pleasant than to sit in the open air watching the fantastic forests of BC go by, then the lush farmlands, then the arid cattle country of rattlesnakes and tumbleweed, then over wooden trestle bridges across roaring chasms. The average speed of about 15mph, dictated by the tortuous curves, provided only a gentle zephyr to cool the passenger's brow.

There being no roads through some of this country (and for over 100 miles of the route there is still no public transport) the PGE was the only means of travel,

and the passenger could derive some mild excitement at the 49 stops in the 274 miles to Williams lake. All but 15 of them were 'flagstops', where the waiting passenger stuck a red flat in a slot to halt the train. The system still operates in the same way.

There was also excitement at meal times before the introduction of dining cars. A contract was made with local housewives who fancied themselves as cooks, and the long melancholy hooting of the PGE train would give her warning that a horde of hungry passengers would descend in 15 minutes. Roast beef and Yorkshire pudding, apple pie and cheese, steaming coffee. The train puffed impatiently as the viands were devoured at long tables. Mrs. Myrtle Phillip, who with her husband Alec had walked into Alta Lake on the PGE in 1910, was one of the providers. She still lives at Alta Lake, walking home on the railway tracks. There is no other way.

The often-violent history of British Columbia is represented by some of the names of the stations on the PGE. Echoes of the Gold Rush abound, and there are English names like Ten Downing Street, Britannia, Birkenhead, and Exeter. The last-named is the home of the eccentric Lord Cecil, a big landowner and head of a religious sect. Then there are the sweet-sounding Indian names like Lillooet, Shalalth and Squamish, and a hint of the French voyageurs in Lac La Hache and Porteau.

It was inevitable that a railway with such character attracted employees of colour and romance, and perhaps the greatest individualist, who was working until recently, bore the name of Charlie Midnight, train driver on the PGE who apparently took the phrase Iron Horse very literally. For Charlie wore the blue jeans and Stetson hat of the cowboy as he rode the footplate of the old steam locomotives, and when he had an audience at a local station, had a great act of beating on the boiler of his charge with his hat as if urging greater speed.

Charlie was a romantic man with a family of eleven children. Myrtle Phillip recalls that he petitioned the government to build a school for his brood, but was reminded that the government would only build new schools for a minimum of twelve pupils. On hearing the news, Charlie was filled with paternal ambition for his offsprings' education, and Mrs. Phillip reports that the PGE train never rattled and swayed round the curves faster than on the night Charlie decided, with the assistance of Mrs. Midnight, to fulfil the demands of the Education Department. The locomotive boiler was flailed that night by the Stetson of the engineer. And nine months later a new school was built at a hamlet on the PGE — all the pupils to be Midnights. Roll call must have sounded like the curtain call of Act II, Cinderella.

(Mrs. Phillip, incidentally, was not only a good provider but was frequently called on by the Indians to assist when little Indians were imminent. There are countless girls called Myrtle on the PGE, and innumerable Alecs.)

The PGE was in a position to give substantial help to the Port of Vancouver this spring when landslides blocked both the Canadian Pacific and Canadian National lines in the notorious Fraser canyon. In Vancouver harbour were 20 ships awaiting cargoes of grain for China, and the elevators were empty. The PGE makes contact with the Canadian National at Prince George, and the vital trains were diverted on to PGE track, which avoids the Fraser canyon.

Premier W. A. C. Bennett of BC claims: 'There is no railway in all of North America which can approach the PGE's prodigious growth through new line construction.' Carloadings have increased 70 per cent in the past ten years, and an equal or bigger rate of growth is forecast in the next decade as the line reaches out to the north to tap an abundance of forest and mine resources, deposits of coal, silver, lead, zinc, copper and jade.

Far left: A BC Hydro trolleybus outside the PGE offices in Vancouver. V Goldberg

Left: PGE northbound passenger and southbound logging trains pass at a mountain halt. V Goldberg

Below: Multiple diesel heading is typical of present PGE operations, as the bridge location is typical of the country through which it passes.
British Columbia Railway (R Wild)

Tracklaying in the bitter winter is a study of men struggling to keep up with the pace of a machine. The main equipment is a travelling crane that inches along the track as it is laid. The crane lifts forward the ties (sleepers) to a gang of 30 men, then transfers to them the rails from the supply wagons trailing behind. Rate of progress is one mile a day, laid on ballast already prepared. Behind the supply wagons come the sleeping cars and kitchens for the crew. It is a compact organisation.

But, watching the operation on a ten-below-zero day this winter, the writer noticed that the gang's foreman used hand signals rather than spoken orders. 'There's about ten nationalities among the 30 men,' he said. 'Some of them talk hardly any English. But they understand one Canadian tradition — overtime. They don't want to stop unless it's 20 below . . .'

For its first 12½ miles, the PGE runs through the dormitory suburbs of North and West Vancouver before launching itself along the shores of Howe sound and into the lonely interior. In North Vancouver, the track is confined to industrial property, but when the train crosses the Capilano river into West Vancouver, a truly remarkable situation emerges. For the railway company, after running through the largely unoccupied suburbs from 1915 to 1921, suddenly quit working as if in a sulk, tore up the tracks, and confined its operation to the interior, lack of money being the reason. The railhead was now 40 miles away at Squamish, at the far end of Howe sound, and the freight was shipped on to barges at Squamish for the transfer to Vancouver. The railroad had no competition from road transport from Vancouver to Squamish and beyond, and the residents at the little hamlets along the way for over 100 miles, mostly Indians, had no means of moving other than by the PGE.

Passengers used the water, crowded on a picturesque steamer called the *Bonnybelle,* between Vancouver and Squamish. But the PGE, in the tradition of railroads, retained the right-of-way through North and West Vancouver, a single track along the shoreline. Between the Company's retreat in 1921, however, and its decision to return in 1956, all kinds of dramatic things had happened to the city of Vancouver and its environs. It had burst at the seams, for one thing, and one result was the building of the Lion's Gate Bridge from the metropolis to West Vancouver in 1938, opened by King George VI on his last visit to North America before the war.

The bridge connected the city and the suburb over an inlet, and it established West Vancouver as a most desirable dormitory, with excellent property along the rocky coastline. A stretch of beach for every home. A spectacular view of famed Stanley park from every picture-window. It was to become Canada's Golden Coast, the home of lumber barons, stock market millionaires, and the money-elite of the West. Waterfront property soared to $800 a foot. But — there was the PGE right-of-way. The residents had forgotten it.

When, after 35 years, the PGE decided to return to town and rebuild its terminus in North Vancouver, the company found the residents and the builders and landscapers had played fast and loose with the right-of-way. Roses bloomed, peas sprouted, children played in pools,

and dogs had kennels on the PGE property. Some builders, thinking the PGE had gone for ever, built the kitchen door within inches of where locomotives had thundered. In some cases, a housewife was on PGE property when she went out to wash the windows.

The dread day came when the first train used the newly laid track through a forest of shaking fists, rattling the Worcester china in the commodes, inciting innocent children to scream in the night, a searchlight probing into the darkest corners of the Master's den, unsettling the caged budgerigars, the pedigree dogs, and even the burgeoning peony buds. It was Gotterdammerung.

Len Norris, brilliant cartoonist of the 'Vancouver Sun', drew a famous cartoon which showed a hypothetical, almost possible, domestic crisis. Grandma was late for supper again. The scene showed the affluent family in the comfortable dining room sitting in silence, stunned by the 15mph passing of a loaded freight train, giant boxcars runbling within feet of the dining table. But Grandma had planned her strategy without consideration of the PGE. Norris visualised that in the 35 years of peace, this family had built one of its bathrooms the other side of the right-of-way. Grandma was trapped again. It was one of the most popular Norris cartoons on the PGE, most of which became collectors' items.

The PGE survived, despite the pleas of waterfront dwellers who found themselves cut off from their garages, and protests from gardeners who found a railroad's spray control of weeds to be devastating. There were only two passenger trains, one going north at eight in the morning and another returning at ten at night. The long freights were on scheduled programmes, but there was one in the early hours that convulsed the sleeping residents for the ten minutes of its passing. The speed was limited to 15mph and use of the horn in the suburb was prohibited.

There were also dangers. In February 1972 a series of miracles resulted in no deaths or injuries when six loaded box cars jumped the tracks in early morning and rolled down the hillside at a cliffy section of West Vancouver. Two wagons hit the well-travelled road below. One house lost its living room; a month before, that space had been sleeping quarters for a man, wife and two children. One huge van teetered against an arbutus tree, a few feet above a modern house. The speed limit in West Vancouver was forthwith reduced to 10mph. It was indeed the Please Go Easy.

As with most railways in the world, the PGE seems to have been overtaken by events outside its control. From being a lifeline for residents up and down the line, the railway has become a conveyor for containers and wagons of lumber from forests in the interior to factories and ships in the city.

Above: Passenger set and locomotive in old livery at Lillooet in June 1962. M L Hales

Left: A freight train headed north for Fort St John crosses the longest PGE bridge (3,251ft) over Peace River, 700 miles north of Vancouver.
British Columbia Railway (R Wild)

The railway's service to the public, and the public's dependence on the iron link, was perhaps best illustrated by the experience of Mrs. Lucy Markham of West Vancouver, who proudly claims to have been the first white child born on the PGE. The historic event was in the days before 1921 when the line served, in the absence of a road, the area that is now the suburb of West Vancouver. Mrs. Markham's parents lived at the end of steel, and when it became evident that Lucy was on the way, her mother was hastily carried into a PGE luggage van for an emergency journey to a Vancouver hospital. Lucy didn't wait for the engineer to reach the terminal. She is also the only white child to have been born on the PGE.

The PGE staff seemed to recognise that the railway was an essential part of the community. A few years ago, our teenage daughter was returning home and was due to alight at our local flagstop after dark. The conductor, learning that she would be the only passenger stepping into the night, obtained our telephone number and called from the train to make sure she would be met.

Today, with the coming of fine new highways in British Columbia, except for the 100 miles through the mountains where only the PGE has traversed, there is little passenger traffic on the railway. The train leaves North Vancouver for Prince George on alternate days only, and there are only two or three Budd cars, on which the meals are served at seats as on an aircraft. No more of Myrtle's apple pies. No more sleeping cars on the PGE, for owing to the swift acceleration and braking of the self-propelled Budd cars, the journey to Prince George is completed in 16½ hours between eight o'clock in the morning and half an hour after midnight. There are no more Charlie Midnights, and the temperature control is by thermostat — the pot-bellied stoves long retired, and no more swinging oil lamps.

It will be recognised that the PGE has had its share of troubles, dramas, and victories. But in April of 1972 there was a change of another kind. By order of the Premier of BC, W. A. C. Bennett, who has given the railroad his personal attention, the name Pacific Great Eastern was changed to British Columbia Railway. The last link with Britain had been severed.

The BC Railway will no doubt go on from strength to strength. But sentimental old friends do not easily relinquish an affectionate nickname. Up and down its 1,000 miles, from Britannia to Ten Downing Street to Sundance to Azouzette to Fort St. James, they will still be calling it the Please Go Easy.

Top: A southbound freight takes a siding for the northbound passenger set south of Lillooet in May 1964. V Goldberg

Centre: Alco-type MLW locomotive No 569 at Lillooet. V Goldberg

Left: Heavy freight moved over the PGE has increased dramatically in recent years and now employs modern high-power diesels.
British Columbia Railway (R Wild)

Opposite Page: CPR locomotive No 1, 4-4-0 'Countess of Dufferin' at rest outside Winnipeg CP Station. V P Goldberg

THE CPR CANADIAN

Canadian Pacific Railway has a main line 3,363 miles in length which although not unique is still unusual. The CPR main line crosses the continent of North America at its widest from Saint John, New Brunswick, on the Bay of Fundy, to Vancouver, British Columbia, on the Pacific. Actually this immense mileage is shared between the rival Canadian National Railway, which from Halifax on the Atlantic skirts the head of the Bay of Fundy, and takes a more northerly course across Canada, to become slightly the longer of the two routes between Montreal and Vancouver.

There are no regular through trains between the Atlantic and the Pacific, however; the journey covered by the train indicated in the title runs between Montreal and Vancouver, 2,880 miles, taking not far short of three days in the process. A section of the train starts from Toronto, making a journey shorter by 176 miles, and joins the main train at Sudbury, 435 miles from Montreal.

But first a word or two about the Canadian Pacific Railway, which helped materially in shaping Canadian history. The first proposal for a Canadian trans-continental railway was made by an Imperial Commission as far back as 1857, and a band of explorers spent four years in trying to map out a route. But although they discovered the Kicking Horse Pass (so named humorously because a pack horse kicked a member of the survey party), through which the CPR was eventually to pass, the difficulty posed by the great ranges of the Rockies and the Selkirks caused the leader of the party to report, 'The knowledge of the country as a whole would never lead me to advocate a line of communication from Canada across the continent to the Pacific'. But in 1865 another survey party, organised by the Surveyor-General of British Columbia, carried out a more-detailed exploration, and claimed to have dis-covered a practicable route.

Six more years passed before any further steps were taken. Until that time, Canada had been no more than a loose association of provinces or colonies, generally acknowledging British rule, but one of them at least —

British Columbia — was becoming extremely restive at its lack of communication with the rest of Canada. Indeed, it is not beyond the bounds of possibility that British Columbia might have seceded to the United States had not the building of a trans-continental railway come urgently under review. The task to be faced was immense — first the rocky out-crops muskegs and swamps in the almost uninhabited country west of Ottawa before Lake Superior could be reached; then some difficult construction round the cliffs bordering the lake; after that hundreds of miles across prairie country to the great chain of the Rockies west of Calgary in Alberta; and finally 500 miles of track loca-tion and laying through fearsome mountain country.

How the task was tackled would itself require one or more books adequately to describe, and at one stage the work nearly came to a standstill through lack of money. The Canadian Pacific Railway was incorporated in February 1881 and before the end of the century included in its corporate structure many railways in the provinces of Ontario and Quebec which had been in existence from the 1850s onwards. The new CPR, with the support of the Canadian government, began pushing eastwards and westwards from Winnipeg with such vigour that in no more than four years — five years before the obligatory date of completion of the railway — rail communication was established throughout between Montreal, on the St. Lawrence river, and Vancouver, British Columbia.

With the financial assistance of a number of distin-guished men, and the driving power of William Van Horne, the laying of the line proceeded apace in both directions, and on November 5, 1885, the two tracks met at Craigellachie, in the heart of the Gold Range, where the last spike was driven. Such was the necessity of completing the railway before funds ran out that in the 18 months from May 1882, no less than 675 miles of track were laid across the undulating prairies to the junction of the Bow and Elbow rivers — the future site of Calgary — with a maximum of 6 miles 660 yards in a

single day.

On May 23, 1887, the first Canadian Pacific Railway train from the east ran into Vancouver. The 1½-year interval since completion had been occupied in improving the hastily laid track so that trains could make the through journey safely Because it had been essential to get the service going at the earliest possible moment, a good deal of the original construction, especially through the three ranges of the Rocky Mountains, was of a rather temporary nature. The intention was to replace the temporary structures by others of a permanent character as soon as the railway was earning money and adequate time could be given to the reconstructions. Over many mountain ravines the railway was carried on great timber trestle viaducts, fabricated from timber cut in the adjacent forests. The greatest of the trestle viaducts was across Stoney Creek, later replaced by a massive steel arch.

Some of the improvements were more costly. After the line had dropped from the Kicking Horse Pass down to the gorge of the Columbia River at Golden, it was felt that to follow the river's great bend to the northwards would mean too great a diversion, so a route was taken through the Selkirk Mountains to reach the river again at Revelstoke. It involved a tortuous climb on 1 in 45 gradients to the 4,350ft altitude of the Rogers Pass, 4½ miles of which had to be protected by timber snowsheds in order to avoid blockage of the line by snow in the winter months. The bold decision was reached later to cut out the difficult section by tunnelling under Mount Macdonald. This 5-mile bore lowered the railway's summit by 540ft and, for a cost of £1,125,000, vastly improved the operating over the section when the Connaught Tunnel was opened in 1916.

Another costly improvement affected the descent westwards down the Yoho Valley from the 5,329ft altitude of the Great Divide. For speed of construction

the original line was carried straight down the valley on a ruling gradient of 1 in 23, which proved a serious handicap to trains having to climb in the eastbound direction, while in the westbound direction care was needed to prevent trains from running away down so steep an inclination. An entirely new location therefore was devised, reducing the gradient from 1 in 23 to 1 in 45, and was brought into use in 1909. On the new route trains starting the descent enter a spiral tunnel from which they emerge at a level lower by 54ft, travelling in the opposite direction. After crossing the river and the former route, which is now a road, they enter a similar tunnel in the opposite mountainside to emerge at a still lower level heading in the original direction. The relocation has added several miles to the distance covered, of course, but halving the steepness of the descent has made all the difference to the operation. The route closely resembles that familiar to European travellers at Wassen on the Gotthard Railway of Switzerland.

Against the general trend of decline, almost to extinction, of inter-city rail passenger travel in North America, the Canadian (in parallel with the rival Canadian National Super Continental) continues to provide a very high standard of service across the width of Canada between Montreal and Vancouver. Until recently, the Canadian's 'list of equipment' included in the CPR timetable showed that the train consist included scenic-dome coffee shop; stainless steel sleepers with drawing rooms, compartments, bedrooms, roomettes, duplex roomettes, and standard berths; stainless steel streamlined coaches with reserved seats; and dining room car.

Drawing rooms, compartments and bedrooms are self-contained sleeping rooms commanding supplements to the first-class fare varying with their size; Duplex roomettes are smaller sleeping compartments dovetailed into one another. Standard berths are of the older type, in which pairs of seats each side of a central gangway are drawn together to form lower berths, and the ceilings on each side are let down to provide upper berths, curtains being drawn along the aisle side of both to provide a measure of privacy. Coaches are the equivalent of British second class, with reclining seats which can be tilted at night to the near horizontal for sleeping comfort.

As to traction, during the days of steam the Canadian Pacific Railway developed locomotives of very considerable power. On a journey of such length locomotives needed, of course, to be changed at a number of division points, and their crews more frequently still. Exceptional power was essential with passenger trains which, in later years, frequently were comprised of as many as 15 coaches of heavy North American stock, perhaps up to 900 tons in weight.

As train weights increased, locomotive design progressed through 4-6-2 and 4-8-2 types to a culmination in two outstanding designs – a 4-6-4 or Hudson type for the flatter sections, capable of working continuously over distances approaching 1,000 miles and, for the mountain section, an extremely powerful 2-10-4 design. The Hudsons worked the Canadian through over the 980-odd miles between Montreal and Fort William, on Lake Superior, and over the 832 miles between Winnipeg and Calgary. They had 6ft 3in coupled wheels, 22in by 30in cylinders, 80.8sq ft firegrate area, 3,861sq ft heating surface and 1,640sq ft superheating surface; working pressure was 275lb per sq in and they weighed 163 tons in working order, or 295 tons with the 12-wheel tenders.

The 2-10-4s, which first appeared in 1929, had 5ft 3in coupled wheels, 25in by 32in cylinders, a firegrate area of 93.5sq ft, 5,054sq ft heating and 2,032sq ft superheating surface, 285lb pressure, and a weight in working order of almost exactly 200 tons. The 12-wheel tenders, which could carry 12,000 gallons of water and 4,100 gallons of fuel oil (they were oil-fired) weighed 127 tons. Yet even such monsters required to be double-headed when climbing the 1 in 45 gradients from Revelstoke up to the Kicking Horse Pass and a fleet of 30 of them were needed to maintain the service.

Since then, however, the all-conquering diesels have taken over, and two or three diesel-electric locomotives in multiple handle the toughest assignments without difficulty. A great advantage of diesel traction is that the risk of forest fires started by steam power has now been eliminated.

The Canadian crossing Stony Creek bridge in British Columbia. C P Rail

The Canadian today takes a nominal 68 hours 35 minutes on its westbound run, but actually 71 hours 35 minutes because of the three changes of time en route; travelling east the journey is 70 minutes shorter. The speed might seem no more than moderate, but as it is the only daily passenger train over the route, it makes no fewer than 37 regular stops, which are allowed in aggregate five hours 35 minutes, giving a net running time of 66 hours. There are also 30 conditional stops when required. Many of the point-to-point runs are made at start-to-stop speeds well in excess of 50mph.

Westbound, the start from Montreal's Windsor station is at 13.55, and after halts to pick up passengers at Westmount, Montreal West and Dorval, there is some fast running over the first 109 miles to the capital, Ottawa. At 23.40, the train rolls into Sudbury, an important junction 435 miles from Montreal, where it is joined by the through section which has left Toronto, 260 miles away, at 17.15. The Sudbury stop, 50 minutes, is the longest on the journey, and the Canadian is not due to leave until 30 minutes after midnight.

By breakfast time next day the train has reached White River, and at Heron Bay, 791 miles from Montreal, passengers catch their first sight of the great inland sea Lake Superior. After a little less than 24 hours from Montreal, at 14.20, the Canadian stops for 15 minutes at Thunder Bay (987 miles), the present name for the former Fort William-Port Arthur, with its great elevators to which the railway brings to grain for shipment from the prairies of Manitoba. Watches are there set back one hour, from Eastern to Central time. For the next 475 miles, to Portage la Prairie, beyond Winnipeg, the track, up to this point single, becomes double — an unusual feature of any North American transcontinental line.

At the great city of Winnipeg, 1,406 miles from the start, it is again time for bed (22.15 to 22.45), and the second breakfast aboard may coincide with stops at towns with such Red Indian names as Moose Jaw, Swift Current and Medicine Hat; Swift Current sees the second watch adjustment, from Central to Mountain time. At the end of the second complete day, at 14.25, the train reaches Calgary, 2,239 miles from the start, with a 35-minute wait in prospect. Incidentally, the variations in altitude so far have been 110ft at Montreal, 1,412ft at Chapleau, 617ft at Thunder Bay, 1,486ft at Ignace, 772ft at Winnipeg, and then a gradual and almost uninterrupted ascent to 3,439ft at Calgary. But the foot-

hills of the Rockies are now in sight ahead and climbing is to begin in earnest.

The line makes for the Bow River valley, which it mounts until it reaches the important town of Banff (2,322 miles, 4,534ft). Still further climbing lies ahead, past Lake Louise with its famous Canadian Pacific Chateau Lake Louise Hotel in a scenic setting, to the maximum altitude of 5,329ft at the Great Divide in the Kicking Horse Pass. The 'Divide', of course, is between the Atlantic and the Pacific watersheds, and at that point, visible from the train, there is a stream which is divided by concrete channels into two parts, one to flow eastwards so that its waters finish in Hudson's Bay, and the other westwards to be carried by the Columbia River into the Pacific.

Then follows the 1 in 45 descent of the Yoho Valley spirals to Field (4,072ft), an important divisional point (where the third watch adjustment is made, from Mountain to Pacific time) and from there to Golden and on down the Columbia River Valley for 63 miles to Beavermouth, at 2,532ft altitude. There the line turns due west to climb through the Selkirks to the Connaught Tunnel, at 3,800ft altitude, before another very steep descent, over 22 miles to Revelstoke, where the Columbia River is rejoined and crossed after its lengthy bend to the northwards. Through the Eagle Pass alongside various lakes the line proceeds until it reaches the valley of the South Thompson River, which is joined at Kamloops by the North Thompson River.

From the north down the North Thompson River runs the line of the great transcontinental competitor, the Canadian National Railway, which as the former Canadian Northern was carried across Canada by the route formerly proposed for the CPR but rejected as being too circuitous, by way of Edmonton and through the Yellowhead Pass. From Kamloops the two lines continue for 250 miles along opposite mountainsides of the same gorge, with scarcely any connection between them. The final stage, for 156 miles from Lytton, is down the gorge of the swiftly flowing Fraser River, in which, just beyond Lytton at Cisco, the two lines change sides, on big steel bridges, the CPR from then on taking the right bank. Finally, with the comfort of bed sought for the third night aboard for the through passenger, at about Revelstoke, there is ample time for breakfast before the Canadian comes to rest at 10.30 on the third morning, at the end of its memorable journey of 2,880 miles from Montreal.

Right: CPR diesel No 1408 heading the eastbound Canadian at Field, BC, In May 1964. V Goldberg

Below: CP Rail's trans-continental train, the Canadian, approaching Lake Louise, near Banff, with the Rockies in the background. CP Rail

Right: A roomette on the Canadian. CP Rail

TOURIST RAILWAYS IN AMERICA

Tourist Railway is a description which covers several varieties of operating railways in each of which the railway itself forms a major attraction, while transportation, the service which railways usually provide, generally plays a lesser role. The annual directory of tourist railways in America has rapidly expanded during the relatively few years in which it has been published, and today contains upwards of one hundred entries. The tourist railways are now part of an extensive leisure industry, and are expanding in number.

Tourist railways can be divided into several categories. There are those which operate in scenic areas, where the train itself originally attracted only modest attention. Mountain cog lines are in this class. Then there are those lines operating vintage equipment, particularly steam locomotives. Their attractions are increased if they run in scenic areas, or near a tourist resort. Several such lines are to be found near major cities — they provide a variation in the recreational activities available to the city dwellers. Some lines of this type operate over the tracks of working railroads, which haul revenue freight on weekdays and carry tourist passengers at weekends.

Another form of tourist attraction is the railway museum display; generally, these were conceived as static exhibits, but experience has shown that operation of rail vehicles adds greatly to the attractions of such collections, as well as providing a very necessary additional source of revenue for meeting the continuing needs of maintenance. A further variety in this class is the trolley museum, where street railway cars or interurbans operate on short lengths of track equipped with overhead wire. In several instances, trolley museums utilise the former rights-of-way of discontinued interurban lines, the track having been laboriously relaid by volunteers in their leisure time.

The term tourist railway might also be applied to lines laid out in amusement parks, as one of a number of types of 'adventure' or 'nostalgia' attractions. Disney-

Below left: Manitou & Pike's Peak 4-4-0T No 4 at Colorado Railroad Museum at Denver. C M Whitehouse

This picture: Victoria Pacific Rly 2-8-2 with a train at Millstream junction, near Victoria, BC, in August 1972. V Goldberg

land in California and the new Disney World in Florida are two examples, of a very high standard, of such lines. Unhappily, this category also includes some rather horrible specimens, of which the term fake is a courteous description. Sometimes there is an imported steam locomotive — perhaps a continental European industrial design, in appearance particularly un-American

— making endless circuits of a small circle of tracks, hauling a gaudily-painted train past a series of cheap-jack 'authentic replicas' of vintage bric-a-brac, providing the owner with an ill-deserved living.

The larger operations necessarily are run on commercial lines, although owners are showing an increasing awareness where the equipment in use is of special

historic or technical merit. The smaller operations sometimes depend on a combination of commercial and volunteer support. Restoration of exhibits, other than those actually needed for operation, can absorb considerable amounts of labour, fortunately met from the ranks of dedicated enthusiasts. The larger trolley museums are dependent almost entirely on voluntary labour.

Perhaps here is the point to express some concern at the many items of great historic value which are either in private hands, or in the hands of informal groups. Relatively few exhibits have the stability of public ownership with a professional museum staff, and an attendant budget, to ensure safe preservation for posterity. That the problem is appreciated by present owners is evidenced by the several museum trusts that exist. such trusts however are often sadly lacking in funds such as the great foundations accord to the Arts, for example. The increasing interest in preserving the past should nevertheless ensure that the necessary funds can continue to be raised in the future.

So much, then, for a rather formal, analytical, look at the generalities of the tourist railway. Let us turn to some examples. One of the oldest tourist railways is undoubtedly the cog railway which ascends Mount Washington in northern New Hampshire. Although the rack system was used in the earliest days of railways to supplement adhesion — Blenkinsop patented a system in 1811 — the Mt Washington line claims to pre-date the now numerous Swiss systems, and in 1969 passed its century. The line ascends from its base station (at 2,569ft) to the summit (6,288ft) in $3\frac{1}{3}$ miles. The gradient averages nearly 1 in 4, and at its steepest exceeds 1 in 3. The line's gauge is variously quoted as 4ft 7½in and 4ft 8in. It is to this day worked by steam. The locomotives are carried on four flanged wheels, but the drive from four cylinders, arranged in two pairs, is through jackshafts on to cogs engaging in a ladder-type rack. A brand-new steam locomotive joined the existing fleet of seven (some dating from 1870) in 1972.

The other major cog railway is that up Pike's Peak in Colorado — a line of more recent construction. It is of standard gauge and ascends from the lower terminus at Manitou Springs, 6,562ft (about 70 miles South of Denver) to the summit at 14,109ft, in 8.9 miles. The line was steam powered until the nineteen-fifties, but is now worked by several General Motors diesel units, and in addition some more recently built Swiss railcars. At least four of the steam locomotives have been preserved; apart from their interest as cog locomotives, they are thought to be the last extant examples of Vauclai compounds.

Not far from Manitou Springs is the very select Broadmoor hotel; from an ice rink near the hotel, a third American cog railway, of 3ft gauge, climbs a two-mile course to a zoo. Its sole motive power is a Cadillac-powered tractive unit, which draws two trailer cars. The line lacks any switches or sidings — there is just a single running line; and hourly service is provided during the season.

The western half of the State of Colorado, the heart of the Rocky Mountains, is a major tourist area; it is not surprising, therefore, to find a number of other tourist railways within a 250-mile radius of Denver (the state, be it remembered, measures about 400 miles by 300

miles). By far the best known of all the lines which we shall mention is the Silverton, and not without justification. It dates from 1882.

The 45-mile run from Durango to Silverton follows the Animas river throughout its length. It rises from 6,502ft elevation at Durango to 9,302ft at Silverton and at its most spectacular point, peaks in the San Juan mountains rise to 14,000ft. The view from the narrow canyon is spectacular indeed, and at one point the train edges its way past the Pallisades on a narrow ledge with a sheer drop to the river below. The trains are just as fascinating (for much of the season two trains run); some of the cars still in use date back to the 1880s, and steam haulage continues behind 3ft-gauge 2-8-2 locomotives built in 1923, using coal mined locally.

From twice-weekly mixed-train operation which survived the 1939-45 war, the line gradually became more widely known, initially because of its scenery. Between 1953 and 1957, traffic doubled and now, over 100,000 passengers are carried in each four-month season (effectively the end of May to the beginning of October). The Denver & Rio Grange Western Railroad is the operator.

It might be thought that little could match this line, but it is now complemented by the Cumbres & Toltec Scenic Railroad, which follows a serpentine 64-mile route along the Colorado-New Mexico state line from Chama, NM, 100 miles east of Durango, to Antonito, Colo. The line once formed part of the link between the Silverton and the remainder of the D&RGW system at Alamosa.

Still in Colorado, and only about 40 miles west of Denver, is the Colorado Central Narrow Gauge Railway. It is at present quite short and is laid to 3ft gauge on the old track-bed of an earlier Colorado & Southern narrow-gauge line in Central City, once a gold mining town. It has recovered from its later 'ghost-town' status by catering for the tourist, to whom the CCNG is a major attraction. The line is operated by two American-built 2-8-0s brought back to the USA after about 50 years' service in Central America.

Between Central City and Denver lies Golden, a small town on the outskirts of which has been established the Colorado Railroad Museum. It is primarily static, with a number of full-size exhibits and a great quantity of printed and written material, most of which originated from within the state. Just occasionally, a locomotive is steamed with the help of some of the local volunteer enthusiasts.

Opposite Page. A reproduction of an American 0-4-0 at Disneyland, California. D J Kingston

This Page: Locomotive No 8 built in 1880 for the Washington COG Railway. P B Whitehouse

Colorado is a state which the tourist is reluctant to leave, but we must now look at some of the other tourist railways; New England is a suitable starting point for the east. About 40 miles south-east of Boston is South Carver, Mass (not far from the famous Plymouth Rock), where the Edaville Railroad is located. The line takes its name from the initials of Ellis D Atwood, its founder, but its origins go back to the State of Maine. Several railways of purely local interest were built in southern Maine to the very narrow gauge of 2ft, which was very rare elsewhere until about 1944. Although they were all scrapped, a number of items of equipment survived. Mr Atwood gathered whatever he could, and in 1946-47 laid out a 5½ mile circuit of track on a cranberry bog at the base of Cape Cod. Intended at first as an adjunct to cranberry farming, the railway carried passengers on a courtesy basis, but increasing crowds of visitors quickly led to the establishment of scheduled services during the summer season, Full-size standard-gauge and model displays were added, as well as a museum building and restaurant, and today Edaville is a major New England tourist attraction.

Unhappily, its founder was killed in an accident in 1950, and in 1955 the railway passed to F Nelson Blount who developed the operation on its existing site. By sad coincidence, Mr Blount was also killed in an accident in 1967, when his private plane crashed during an emergency landing. Fortunately, the Edaville is still in good hands today. Mr Blount's name is also linked with another major New England attraction – Steamtown USA. Steamtown is a static display with over 40 locomotives, located close to the Connecticut river, which forms the Vermont – New Hampshire border, at Bellows Falls. Associated with Steamtown is the Green Mountain

Railroad, a freight-only carrier which operates over the former Rutland Railroad tracks. There in the summer, steam trains run again for tourists, from Riverside (near Bellows Falls) to Chester, 11 miles. The regular locomotive is an ex-Canadian Pacific lightweight 4-6-2 of recent (1948) build, hauling ex-commuter coaches (often favoured by tourist lines because of their high seating capacity) from the Central Railroad of New Jersey.

Lower down the Connecticut river, at Essex, Con, is another steam tourist line, the Valley Railroad, which operates over a 4-mile-long section of a former New Haven Railroad branch line. The usual motive power is a compact 2-6-2, from the Sumter & Choctaw Railway, in Alabama. There is also a 2-8-0 from the Birmingham & Southeastern. The usual ex-commuter coaches provide working rolling stock, and there are several additional vehicles, including a dining car, a Pullman sleeper and a Railway Post Office car, on display. The exhibits are the property of the Empire State Railway Museum, located in the mid nineteen-sixties at Middletown, NY, about 66 miles from New York City. There, the tracks of the freight-hauling Middletown & New Jersey Railway were used at week-ends for seasonal tourist operations, but the subsequent inauguration of steam tourist trains on the Morris County Central Railroad, only 30 miles from metropolitan New York, resulted in discontinuance of pleasure rides on the M & NJ.

There are several other tourist lines in New York. Two of them are located in the Western extremity of the state. The Arcade & Attica Railroad and the Livonia Avon & Lakeville Railroad, which supplements the modest living which it earns as a diesel-operated freight carrier on weekdays by carrying tourist passengers be-

hind a 2-8-0 engine of 1927 vintage at weekends. The line is located in the so-called Finger Lake region of New York State, an area of rolling country interspersed with long narrow lakes.

Returning to the heavily populated New York – Philadelphia area, there are to be found several other tourist lines which provide vintage train rides. About halfway between the two cities is the Black River & Western Railroad, based on Ringoes, NJ (not far from the state capital, Trenton). Weekday freight service (diesel-hauled) between Ringoes and Flemington (12 miles) is over a former Pennsylvania Railroad branch line, now in independent hands, and weekend steam tourist service is provided using a 2-8-0 formerly on the Great Western Railway (of Colorado), or by a handsome light Pacific from the Florida East Coast line. In the high season — July and August — the steam trains run on certain weekdays as well; an interesting facility is the inclusion in a diesel-hauled weekday freight train of some vehicles to accommodate any passengers who might be interested. Once again, ex-commuter coaches from the Jersey Central carry the passengers, while other exhibits include an 1854 station.

Nearer to Philadelphia is the New Hope & Ivyland Railroad. Once again freight trackage of a small, now independent, line is used for steam tourist trips, with former Canadian National 4-6-0 No 1533 in use. The line is a former branch of the Reading System, and like both its parent and its bigger neighbour, Penn Central, it is bankrupt, but nevertheless continues both freight and seasonal passenger operations.

About 65 miles west of Philadelphia is the 4½mile-long Strasburg Railroad. It branches off the busy PC (ex-Pennsylvania RR) main line not far from Lancaster, Pa, and has several locomotives used in turn on its steam tourist trips. It is one of the oldest, and also busiest, tourist lines in the USA. Except for the Christmas — New Year period, there is at least weekend service throughout the year, and at busy times, two trains are in daily service. The line is well run, primarily on a commercial basis, with a large well-kept historical display of its own. One of its most interesting locomotives is a small 0-4-0 tender engine, built in 1905, which came from a Colorado Fuel & Iron Co plant. It is claimed to be the last operating Camelback, the type of locomotive fitted with a driving cab usually atop the boiler, in front of a wide firebox, and a platform or abbreviated cab behind for the firemen only.

Adjacent to the Strasburg RR is the Railroad Museum of Pennsylvania. It is based on the Pennslvania RR Historic Collection and includes 19 steam locomotives and 12 passenger cars, one of the best such specialist displays in the USA. Of additional interest to visitors to the Strasburg RR is its location in Pennsylvania Dutch country. This is an area settled by members of the Mennonite sect, who eschew most things mechanical and continue to live a simple agricultural life.

About 80 miles west of Lancaster, beyond Harrisburg, lies one of the coal-mining areas of Pennsylvania. There, from the small town of Orbisonia, a 3ft-gauge former coal-carrying line now hauls tourist passengers along a 5-mile route in the verdant Aughwick valley. Four 2-8-2 locomotives are available, all natives to the area, having been built by Baldwin between 1911 and 1918 for the East Board Top Railroad; the name has been kept for the tourist railcar, and an extensive work-

Opposite Page: No 4 'Dixieland' and train of open trucks approaching Bear Mountain on the Roaring Camp & Big Trees line at Felton, California, in October 1971. P J Lynch

This Page: California Western RR 2-8-2 No 45 (Baldwin 1924) at Fort Bragg in August 1972. V Goldberg

ing steam maintenance facility. The EBT was unusual in accepting standard-gauge freight wagons in interchange service over its narrow-gauge line, by exchanging trucks (bogies) at the junction point. Interest in the EBT area is supplemented by the Shade Gap Electric Railway, which adjoins the EBT terminal. The SGER operates electric cars on a mile of standard-gauge track laid on the formation of a branch of the original EBT narrow-gauge line.

One more Eastern line demands notice, the Cass Scenic Railroad. It is located in a rather remote area about 160 miles west and south of Washington DC, close to the Virginia-West Virginia border. The 11 miles of standard-gauge track in use are, unusually, owned by the State of West Virginia, which purchased the former logging line for use as a tourist attraction partly as an unemployment relief project in a depressed area. The line takes a steeply graded (1 in 8 in parts) route, including reversing switchbacks, to the summit of Bald Knob mountain. All three types of geared locomotive are represented six Shays, and one each Heisler and Climax.

Bottom: A two-truck geared loco of White Mountain Central RR preserved at Clarks Trading Post, Lincoln, NH. V Goldberg

Top: Preserved Manitou & Pike's Peak Rly Vauclain compound cog locomotive No 5. V Goldberg

We must now reluctantly skip a number of tourist railway operations located in the US Mid-West — several within reach of Chicago — to visit some of the tourist lines on the Pacific Coast. Many of them are associated with the logging industry, and the Roaring Camp & Big Trees Railroad is typical of half-a-dozen such lines which can be reached from San Francisco. Located about 50 miles south of that city, it is one of the few lines that can be easily reached by public transport — by bus to Felton. The line owns both Shay and Heisler geared locomotives, and in its 2½ miles ascends grades of 1 in 12½, with horseshoe curves and a sizeable trestle bridge, as it winds through the redwoods.

About 140 miles north of San Francisco is the California Western Railroad, with 40 miles of standard-gauge line extending from Fort Bragg on the coast inland through the redwood forest to Willits. Unlike most of the other lines mentioned, the CW has continuously maintained passenger service since its completion early in the century. In more recent years, passengers have been carried in a variety of distinctly vintage railcars, whose smokey exhaust fumes earned them the soubriquet Skunks. Tourists supplemented the passengers on the line as the scenic attractions of the route became known, and eventually the line restored steam passenger excursion service in season under the title Super Skunk. Such has been the demand that the railcars continue to run as well. A chunky 2-8-2, built by Baldwin in 1924, has been the mainstay of the Super Skunk for some years, although a relatively small Maller articulated 2-6-6-2 built by Baldwin 1937 has been obtained recently. The railcars themselves are of some interest, being of several older designs.

All told, California has over a dozen tourist lines. One with only occasional passenger service, though in daily use both as a freight hauler and with a static display is the Sierra Railroad. Located about 100 miles east of San Francisco, the line will be known, unwittingly, to millions of television and cinema viewers, for it is in frequent use for TV series and films requiring old-time trains for Western dramas.

Finally, let us turn briefly to Canada, where the tourist railway concept is just catching on. One of the newest such operations is on the Pacific Coast, in the outskirts of Victoria on Vancouver Island. The Victoria Pacific started operations in 1972, using three miles of Canadian National Railways track which had latterly been out of use. An oil-fired 2-8-2 from a logging railway provides motive power for two ex-Canadian Pacific commuter coaches, and hourly rides are given during the season.

Just outside Winnipeg, Man, the Prairie Dog Central operates at weekends over a CNR freight line. The operation uses a British-built 4-4-0 (Dubs, 1882) of CPR ancestry, hauling four vintage wooden cars over a 7½ mile route. Eastern Canada might soon have its own tourist railway if the plans of the Credit Valley Railway fructify. It will operate out to Georgetown, about 30 miles west of Toronto. Already, ex-CPR 4-6-0 No 1057 has been earmarked, and a number of period passenger cars have been acquired for seasonal use.

Such, then, are a few of the many tourist lines now in operation in North America. Because of them, restorable old steam locomotives, recently considered only for scrap, have once again become highly desirable properties.

Top: Base station of the Mt Washington Cog Railway in September 1969, with the line's preserved No 1 vertical boiler engine, 'Old Peppersass' in the foreground. P B Whitehouse

Centre: An American type 4-4-0 specially built for use at Disneyland, California. D J Kingston

Below: Ex-D & RGW 3ft-gauge 2-8-2 No 483 on the Cumbres & Toltec Scenic RR, at Antonito, Colo, in August 1972. V Goldberg

COWICHAN VALLEY RAILWAY

Vancouver Island, the largest island off the Pacific coast of North America is about 280 miles long and 50 miles wide. Most of the settlement on the island is on the south and east coasts, and the largest ·city, Victoria, is located at the southermost tip. The island has extensive softwood forests, and harvesting them on a sustained-yield basis is the major industry. The movement of timber for lumber and pulpwood provided the reason for the construction of most of the 2,000 miles of railway which at one time or another have been built, and subsequently taken up, on the island.

It is not surprising, therefore, that the Forest Museum near· Duncan, 40 miles North of Victoria, has many exhibits of railway interest. The grounds of the museum are encircled by about 1½ miles of 3ft-gauge railway, laid out in the shape of a figure of eight. Passengers are carried in two coaches whose bodies are conversions of old highway buses, mounted on former logging trucks (bogies). Usual motive power is one of the 0-4-0T locomotives listed below.

The working locomotives (except the Plymouth) are now all oil-fired (using diesel fuel), and can be (indeed, are) operated by one man. Much the most interesting locomotive is the. Shay. It is mounted on two or three bogies and powered by three vertical cylinders to the right of the offset boiler, just ahead of the cab. Each axle is gear-driven through a jointed shaft. The design provided a very rugged flexible unit with great pulling power, albeit at low speed, fully suited to the steeply graded and roughly laid light track generally found on logging railways. Such operations would often comprise a semi-permanent main line, usually following a river valley, from which temporary spur lines would be laid on the ground into the local area where timber was being cut. From there, the railway was used to carry timber either direct to the lumber mill, or to navigable water, whence it could be towed to a mill.

Shay locomotives were once in widespread use in most of the areas of North America where lumbering was carried out. Two other types of geared locomotive also served forest industries. The Climax is represented at Duncan; this type had two cylinders steeply inclined, but in line with the boiler. The pistons drove a crankshaft geared to a central driveshaft driving all axles of a two- or three-truck arrangement. The last type, not represented at Duncan, was the Heisler. Its two cylinders were arranged in a V and transversely mounted ahead of the cab; they powered a central driveshaft, similarly to the Climax.

The Cowichan Valley Railway, which is open from May to September, provides live action amid the otherwise static exhibits of various aspects of the forest industries. It is located in 40 acres of timbered country edging a lake (over an inlet which the trestle in our picture crosses) and provides a splendid reminder of earlier days in British Columbia.

Working Locomotives   (All 3ft gauge)

No	Type	Builder	Builder's No	Date	Remarks
1	2-Truck Shay	Lima	3147	1920	ex Osborne Bay Wharf Co ex Hillcrest Lumber Co
21	B	?	?	?	30-seat Railcar (Ford)
24	0-4-0T	Vulcan	–	1900	12 Tons
25	0-4-0T	Vulcan	–	1910	18 Tons
26	B	Plymouth	–	1926	8 Tons

Locomotives on Display:

No	Type	Builder	Builder's No	Date	Remarks
1	2-Truck Shay	Lima	2475	1911	ex MacMillan-Bloedel Ltd
3	2-Truck Shay	Lima	3262	1924	ex Mayo Lumber Co
9	2-Truck Climax	Climax	1359	1915	ex Hillcrest Lumber Co

Right: A 1967 picture of a preserved 3ft-gauge Shay at Redwoods State Park, California, showing offset boiler. M J Fox

Below: Western Maryland Shay No 6 at work in January 1946. Lima Locomotive Works

Bottom: A three-truck Heisler geared locomotive with central driveline, on the Cass Scenic Railway, W Virginia P B Whitehouse

A Train of the Cowichan Valley Railway seen crossing a trestle over a small lake at the Forest Museum near Duncan, Vancouver Island.

THE LOGGING ENGINES OF CASS

The turn of the century saw the West Virginian farming country at the foot of Back Allegheny mountain quiet and peaceful as it had been for generations; but change was coming fast, and it came in the shape of the Chesapeake & Ohio Railroad. The magic wand that drove the railway was timber and the entire Greenbier watershead was clothed in it — billions of cubic feet of some of the finest timber in America, both hard and soft. The small town of Cass grew round the railhead, and soon crews of imported Italian labourers began to lay ribbons of steel up the sides of the Cheat mountain. From its summit, lines snaked away into the woods of the Cheat and Elk rivers; tracks were rough and often only temporary, and many were so crude that it seemed impossible for a steam engine to operate over them.

But the tough geared engine, conceived by the Michigan inventor Ephraim Shay, is a match for any lumber road. Unlike the conventional steam locomotive, the Shay and its tender have all their wheels as driving wheels. All the wheels are coupled, through gears and shafts, so none can slip unless they all slip, giving the locomotive maximum tractive ability. Vertical cylinders and pistons have the connecting rods coupled to a horizontal crankshaft that drives a reduction gear to give several power strokes per revolution of the driving wheels. As with the low gears of a motor vehicle, this provides greater ability to deal with steep gradients and heavy loads in an engine of given size than conventional direct coupling. The Shay engine had such high tractive efficiency that usually, if an engine came off the road, the crew put down re-railers and it would pull itself on again.

The Spruce Lumber Company owned and worked the whole operation, from cutting and transporting timber to milling and preparing it in final form of planks and boards. The railway also was self-contained, with its own workshops fully capable of repairing the Shays (all twelve of them) no matter what the damage. It even had its own foundry, with more than twelve hundred patterns for parts, and an engine could almost have been built from scratch there.

But within 50 years, in 1942, modern technology doomed the big mills, and lorries doomed the Shays. A large part of the timber area passed into the hands of the Federal Government, and the holdings dwindled to about 65,000 acres on the southern end of Cheat mountain. For eighteen years operations were continued there on a reduced scale, but from the morning of July 1, 1960, no whistle blew at the mill, and no wheel turned.

However, due to the persistence of railfan Russell Baum, the State of West Virginia was persuaded to buy the remaining engines, track, and rolling stock for the conversion of the railway into the tourist attraction it now is, and in June 1963 the Cass Scenic Railroad made its first public run. Today tens of thousands of tourists travel hundreds of miles to ride with the Shays and their half sister, a Heisler, to the top of Bald Knob — a rail trip of 22 miles through the forests taking 4½ hours. The whole town has come to life again, and a piece of yesterday has been kept alive for today. What is perhaps more unusual for America is that it was the State which saved the day and the lame duck has not only survived but is prospering.

Odd-man-out of the Cass locomotive fleet, the Heisler on the way to Cass, WVa, in December 1967.
H Dodge

Overleaf: Cass Scenic Railways' No 7 taking on
water — P B Whitehouse

Two views of Cass Scenic Railway's No 4 three-truck
Shay at Cass station. C M Whitehouse

THE SAN JUAN EXPRESS

The 200-mile stretch of line from Alamosa to Durango was completed in July 1881, and was extended a further 45 miles north from Durango to Silverton in July 1882. The last-named section is the famous Silverton scenic run. The Alamosa-Durango line, for much of its life, was served by a daily passenger train which, in earlier years, ran through to and from Denver; the Denver-Durango run took 27 to 30 hours. Narrow-gauge sleeping cars were included in the train. At first the route to Denver was via the La Veta pass to Walsenburg, thence via Pueblo and Colorado Springs. Conversion of part of the route to standard gauge led to the train being re-routed via the Royal Gorge, Salida, and the San Luis Valley. The new line north from Alamosa, built in 1890, although well over a mile above sea level and in the heart of the mountains, was dead straight for 53 miles.

Subsequent conversion of the Royal Gorge route to standard gauge resulted in a change of train (and gauge) becoming necessary at Alamosa. The Alamosa-Durango train eventually became known as the San Juan Express; the vintage wooden coaches used on it were vestibules in 1937. Rising costs and declining traffic due to improved highways caused the passenger train to be discontinued in January 1951. Freight trains continued to run, but less and less frequently, until the last one was operated in December 1968.

But the narrow-gauge line was not dead. It traverses an area of widely varying scenic attractions — sufficient to rival (or complement) the Silverton as a tourist railway. After much lobbying, the states of Colorado and New Mexico jointly purchased the 64 miles of serpentine track between Antonito and Chama in the summer of 1970.

In September and October of 1970, the rolling stock which was to be used on the revived railway was worked down the three-rail (mixed standard and narrow gauge) line from Alamosa, where much of it had been stored, to Antonito, to be handed over to the Cumbres and Toltec Scenic Railroad (CATS). Stock included nine locomotives, 102 freight cars and 36 pieces of work equipment.

Passengers are now carried in converted freight cars, open sided (what matter with the splendid scenery?) and much work has been done, largely by volunteers, to get track and equipment into operating condition after years of neglect and disuse. Limited services operated in 1971 and were an instant success. Trains began to run four days a week during the summer season in 1972.

From Antonito, the line rises gradually at first, across flat sagebrush-covered country. Later it climbs into wooded foothills, zig-zagging up side valleys to gain height to the rocky Toltec Gorge — with the only two tunnels on the D&RGW narrow gauge — to reach the summit of 10,015ft at Cumbres Pass. From there 14 miles of 1 in 25 grade — a trial for eastbound trains — winds past Windy Point to reach Chama, former division point and now headquarters of CATS. This is a train ride participants will never forget.

Above: A pair of K36s, Nos 483 and 486, making smoke at the head of a freight train in August 1958.

Inset below: No 476 on the Silverton train at Rockwood in August 1955.

Below: The San Juan Express running alongside the Los Animos river, approaching Silverton, with a thunderstorm threatening above the canyon.
Rail Photo Service (B F Cutler)

Overleaf: A special train for the Illini Railroad Club on the Denver and Rio Grande Western Railroad line from Alamosa to Durango in South West Colorado — V Goldberg

ARCADE & ATTICA

RAILROADS

The Arcade & Attica RR is located about 40 miles south of the city of Buffalo, NY. It branches off the Buffalo-Harrisburg line of Penn Central (formerly Pennsylvania RR) at Arcade junction, 36 miles from Buffalo. About 1½ miles from the junction is the small town of Arcade, whence the A&A heads northwards; today, it terminates at North Jara, 12.7 miles from Arcade.

At one time, the A&A went rather further. Some construction work in the area in the 1850s was not at that time completed because of financial troubles and, after a break in interest around the time of the Civil War, a little more work was done in 1873. Eventually, in 1880, the Tonawanda Valley RR opened between Attica — location of a NY State prison — and Curriers. The line was of 3ft gauge and was quickly constructed utilising earthworks of the earlier uncompleted projects.

The TVRR was backed by the Erie RR, and in 1881 the line was opened between Curriers and Arcade (6.8 miles) under the title of Tonawanda Valley Extension Railroad. Under the aegis of the Tonawanda Valley & Cuba RR, the railway was extended in 1882 33.2 miles to Cuba. The TV&C was, in fact, a consolidation of all three sections of line, and three trains each way daily were run over the 59-mile route.

Traffic did not justify so lavish a service; not only was train service reduced but the southernmost 30 miles were abandoned in 1886. The northern end became the Attica and Freedom RR in 1891, and the new company became bankrupt in 1894. Again it was reorganised, as the Buffalo, Attica & Arcade RR. Under the new organisation, the line was reconstructed to standard gauge. Service was resumed in 1895, after a 2-year break, but only between Attica and Arcade. In 1897, a connecting line between Arcade and the Pennsylvania RR at Arcade Junction was completed, but it was destroyed by a flood in 1902.

A new rail link between Arcade and Arcade Junction was built as part of the Buffalo & Susquehanna RR in 1906, but in 1916 the successor to the B&S, the Wellsville & Buffalo RR was abandoned; in the nick of time, in 1917, this second link with the Pennsy was saved and passed to the Arcade & Attica RR, as the BA&A had become.

The A&A had passed into the local ownership of shippers. A small railbus was run for a time, but passenger traffic declined in the late 1920s; those who wished could still ride the mixed (freight) trains, until 1951. The A&A weathered the depression, and was early in the field with diesels, purchasing two small GE 44-tonners in 1941 and 1947 respectively.

Early in 1957, a flood caused a wash-out at the northern end of the line, and as the majority of traffic was over the southern end, trackage north of North Jara was abandoned. Traffic continued to decline, but in 1963 the decision was made to operate steam-hauled excursion trains at weekends. A 2-8-0, No 18 (built by American Locomotive Co as No 62624 in 1920) was obtained from the Boyne City RR in northern Michigan, and was an instant success when it was put into service in 1963. Locomotive No 14 — illustrated on pages 140/141 entered service on the A&A in 1964, and with six second-hand steel open-platform coaches (ex Delaware Lackawanna & Western RR), 40,000 excursionists were carried in 1965. With the excursion business, freight traffic picked up too, so that today, the future for the A&A looks bright.

Above: The A & A's No 18 has been fitted with a melodious steam chime whistle, atop the dome, to add to the nostalgia.
D H Ellsworth

Right: Alco 2-8-0 of the type preserved on the Arcade & Attica, in this case of New York Central Lines in the 1920s.
Ian Allan Library

Below right: Similar to A & A's Baldwin 4-6-0, No 100 of the Duluth, Missabe & Northern company. Ian Allan Library

Below: Souvenir voucher issued to present-day riders on the Arcade & Attica.
V Goldberg

Group Rate 25 or Over

ONE ADULT ROUND-TRIP TICKET

ISSUED BY

Arcade & Attica Railroad Corporation

278 Main Street
Arcade, New York

SOUVENIR COUPON

Your ride from Arcade, New York to Curriers, New York "Behind Steam" has been made possible through the planning and work of the Board of Directors and Employees . . . not to mention the reliability of the railroad's two steamers — No. 14 and No. 18.

As you ride the slightly more than 14 nostalgic miles you will have sufficient opportunity to hear the mellow sounds of the whistle and breathe the sweet scent of soft coal smoke. On your trip you will see prize dairy herds which graze on farm land that has hardly changed since the original road bed

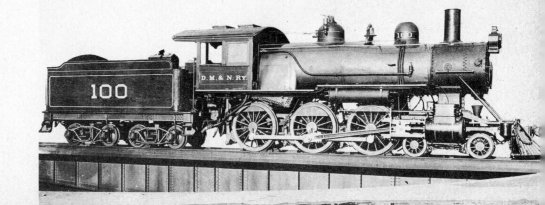

Sperry Rail Service car No 127 on the famed
Horseshoe curve of the former Pennsylvania RR
main line between Harrisburg and Altoona. It is
one of about twenty which patrol the main
routes seeking out metallurgical flaws on the
rails. V Goldberg